Warrior • 101

Roman Auxiliary Cavalryman AD 14–193

Nic Fields • Illustrated by Adam Hook

First published in Great Britain in 2006 by Osprey Publishing,
Midland House, West Way, Botley, Oxford OX2 0PH, UK
443 Park Avenue South, New York, NY 10016, USA
E-mail: info@ospreypublishing.com

A CIP catalogue record for this book is available from the British Library

ISBN 1 84176 973 8

Page layout by Ken Vail Graphic Design, Cambridge (kvgd.com)
Index by Alison Worthington
Originated by United Graphics, Singapore
Printed in China through World Print Ltd.

06 07 08 09 10   10 9 8 7 6 5 4 3 2 1

FOR A CATALOGUE OF ALL BOOKS PUBLISHED BY OSPREY MILITARY AND
AVIATION PLEASE CONTACT:

NORTH AMERICA
Osprey Direct, C/o Random House Distribution Center, 400 Hahn Road,
Westminster, MD 21157
E-mail: info@ospreydirect.com

ALL OTHER REGIONS
Osprey Direct UK, P.O. Box 140 Wellingborough, Northants, NN8 2FA, UK
E-mail: info@ospreydirect.co.uk

Buy online at **www.ospreypublishing.com**

Artist's note

Readers may care to note that the original paintings from
which the colour plates in this book were prepared are
available for private sale. All reproduction copyright
whatsoever is retained by the Publishers. All enquiries
should be addressed to:

Scorpio Gallery
PO Box 475
Hailsham
East Sussex
BN27 2SL

The Publishers regret that they can enter into no
correspondence upon this matter.

CONTENTS

ROMAN AUXILIARY CAVALRYMAN AD 14–193

INTRODUCTION

The army of the early Principate was a professional force of legionaries, auxiliaries and fleet personnel who had enlisted for extended periods of military service and who regarded the army as a definite career. Enlistment was not for the duration of a particular conflict, but for 25 years (26 in the navy), and men were sometimes retained even longer. The loyalty of the army was to the emperor as commander-in-chief, and not to the Senate or the people of Rome.

As part of the military reforms of the first emperor, Augustus (r.27 BC–AD 14), the *auxilia* (auxiliaries) were completely reorganized and given regular status. Trained to the same standards of discipline as the legions, auxiliary soldiers were long-service professionals like the legionaries and served in units that were equally permanent. Drawn from a wide range of warlike peoples throughout the provinces, especially on the fringes of the empire, they were *peregrini* (non-citizens) and would receive Roman citizenship on completion of their 25 years' service. Their senior officers, in contrast, were Roman citizens.

Auxiliaries were a cheaper and, given their primary organization at a lower level (*cohortes* for infantry, *alae* for cavalry), more flexible way of providing the army with the manpower to fulfil its role, especially along Rome's frontiers (Fields 2003B: 40–47). To the *auxilia* fell the tasks of patrolling, containing raids, tax collecting, and the multitudinous duties of frontier troops – the legions were stationed within the frontiers, both to act as a strategic reserve and to intimidate potentially rebellious indigenous 'friendlies'. The *cohortes equitatae* (mixed cohorts) of the *auxilia*, which became increasingly common as the 1st century progressed, encapsulate this flexibility very well. As a combination of foot and horse in a ratio of about 4:1, they were especially suited to garrison and local policing activities, and could hold their own in small-scale warfare.

Roman emperors 27 BC–AD 193						
Iulio-Claudians		**Flavians**			**Antonines**	
27 BC–AD 14	Augustus	AD 69–79	Vespasian		AD 138–161	Antoninus Pius
AD 14–37	Tiberius	AD 79–81	Titus		AD 161–169	Marcus Aurelius and Lucius Verus
AD 37–41	Caius Caligula	AD 81–96	Domitian			
AD 41–54	Claudius	**Adoptive Emperors**			AD 169–180	Marcus Aurelius
AD 54–68	Nero	AD 96–98	Nerva		AD 180–192	Commodus
'Year of Four Emperors'		AD 98–117	Trajan		AD 193	P. Helvius Pertinax
AD 68–69	Galba	AD 117–138	Hadrian			
AD 69	Otho				AD 193	M. Didius Severus Iulianus
AD 69	Vitellius					

CHRONOLOGY

AD 14	Death of Augustus. Rhine-Danube legions mutiny.
AD 14–16	War against Arminius of the Cherusci. Germanicus' victory at Indistaviso.
AD 17–24	Rebellion of Tacfarinas (ex-auxiliary) in Numidia.
AD 19	Arminius murdered by rival chieftains.
AD 21	Gallic revolt.
AD 26	Thracian revolt.
AD 28	Frisii rebel.
AD 40–44	Mauretania rebels; suppressed by C. Suetonius Paulinus.
AD 42	Rebellion of F. Camillus Scribonius, governor of Dalmatia.
AD 43	Claudius conquers southern part of Britannia.
AD 47	Cn. Domitius Corbulo suppresses Frisii.
AD 48	P. Ostorius Scapula, governor of Britannia, crushes Iceni revolt.
AD 51	Ostorius Scapula defeats Caratacus. Silures continue to resist.
AD 55–64	War with Parthia over Armenia. Corbulo captures Artaxata and Tigranocerta.
AD 60	Suetonius Paulinus, governor of Britannia, captures Mona (Anglesey).
AD 60–61	Rebellion of Iceni under Boudicca; suppressed by Suetonius Paulinus.
AD 66–74	Jewish revolt.
AD 67	Vespasian subdues Galilee. Joseph ben Matthias (Josephus) surrenders.
AD 68	Rebellion of C. Iulius Vindex, governor of Gallia Lugdunensis.
AD 68–69	Civil war; 'Year of Four Emperors'.
AD 69	Battles of First/Second Cremona.
AD 69–70	Rebellion of Iulius Civilis (ex-prefect); suppressed by Q. Petilius Cerialis.
AD 70	Titus sacks Jerusalem.
AD 71–73	Petilius Cerialis, governor of Britannia, defeats Brigantes.
AD 73–74	Flavius Silva besieges Masada.
AD 73–77	Sex. Iulius Frontinus, governor of Britannia, defeats Silures.
AD 83	Cn. Iulius Agricola, governor of Britannia, defeats Caledonii at Mons Graupius.
AD 85–89	War with Decebalus of Dacia.
AD 86	Chatti cross Rhine.
AD 89	Rebellion of Antonius Saturninus, governor of Germania Inferior.
AD 101–102	Trajan's first Dacian war.
AD 105–106	Trajan's second Dacian war. Decebalus commits suicide.
AD 114	Rome annexes Armenia.
AD 114–117	Trajan's Parthian war.
AD 115–117	Revolt of Jewish communities in Egypt, Cyrene and Cyprus.
AD 119	Q. Pompeius Falco, governor of Britannia, suppresses revolt of Brigantes.
AD 122	Visit to Britannia by Hadrian; work begins on Hadrian's Wall.
AD 131–135	Rebellion of Bar Kochba in Judaea.
AD 131–137	L. Flavius Arrianus (Arrian) governor of Cappadocia.
AD 138–139	Revolt of northern tribes in Britannia.
AD 142–143	Building of Antonine Wall across Forth-Clyde line.
AD 162–166	War with Parthia over Armenia. Lucius Verus sacks Ctesiphon and Seleucia.
AD 164	Hadrian's Wall re-occupied.
AD 167–180	War with Marcomanni and Quadi on Danubian frontier.
AD 175	Rebellion of Avidius Cassius, governor of Syria.
AD 186	P. Helvius Pertinax, governor of Britannia, suppresses mutiny in province.
AD 192	Commodus assassinated.
AD 193–197	Civil war. L. Septimius Severus emerges victorious.

Trajan's Column (scene CXLV). Tiberius Claudius Maximus, a cavalryman in *ala II Pannoniorum,* captures the dying Decebalus, king of the Dacians. Tiberius' tombstone (*AE* 1969/1970.583) was found near Philippi, and above its biographical inscription is a relief recording this exploit. (Reproduced from Lepper-Frere CVI)

RECRUITMENT

Drawn from peoples nurtured in the saddle, the cavalry of the *auxilia* provided a fighting arm in which the Romans themselves were not so adept. The Romans therefore preferred to recruit former enemies such as the Gauls, Germans, Celtiberians and Thracians, all of whom were renowned for their equestrian skills. As a consequence, Roman equestrian arms, equipment and even tactics were largely borrowed and adapted from 'barbarians'. In spite of its varied origins, however, the Roman cavalry was organized, disciplined and well trained in the Roman manner. Able to skirmish and perform shock action, cavalry were valuable in reconnaissance, communication and policing duties, as well as in battle, when they demonstrated the ability not only to influence its progress, but to make it decisive by turning defeat into rout through a concerted pursuit. As part of the frontier garrisons, however, perhaps their most crucial roles were in reconnaissance and communications.

The Gauls were considered to be the most skilful riders (Strabo 4.4.2) and, as is evident from Table 1, the three Gallic provinces provided some 44.5 per cent of the troopers serving in the cavalry of the *auxilia* during the Flavian period, AD 69–96. It has been estimated that in the time of Augustus the army had a total strength of some 300,000 men, of which around 30,000 were cavalry. By the turn of the 2nd century these figures had risen to approximately 385,000 and 65,000 respectively (Feugère 2002: 133).

Special officers were appointed to collect *tironis* (recruits) in designated areas, while elsewhere commanding officers were normally responsible for recruiting men to the units under their charge. A *probatio* (examination) was held to ensure that recruits were physically fit and legally eligible to serve. The physical standards for the medical examination are not known for our period, but according to Vegetius (1.5), writing after AD 387, the height requirement for recruits joining the cavalry in the early Principate had been 6 Roman feet (5ft 10in or 1.78m), the absolute minimum being 5 Roman feet 10 inches (5ft 8in or 1.73m). Having passed his *probatio*, the *tiro* (recruit) would receive *viaticum* (travelling money) and was then posted to a unit. When he arrived, and before he was entered on the rolls of the unit and allocated to a *turma* (troop), the *tiro* took the *sacramentum* (military oath), swearing loyalty to the emperor. Probably at this time he was issued his *signaculum* ('dog tags'), an inscribed lead tablet worn around the neck in a leather pouch.

The ideal recruit

Vegetius (1.2–7) provides a detailed description of the best type of recruit, including the region he should come from, his previous occupation, age, physical size and fitness, and education. Scholars discussing recruitment have assumed that the average recruit met these high standards, rather than representing an ideal seldom realized in practice (Watson 1985: 37–53; Davies 1989: 3–30; Dixon-Southern 1992: 78–86). A rigorous selection process for recruits is held responsible for the high quality of the Roman army (Davies 1989: 28–30). Yet there is much evidence to overturn this view, thereby suggesting that units could not afford to be so fussy in their selection of

PROVINCE	NUMBER	PERCENTAGE
Gallia Lugdunensis	13,000	33
Hispania Tarraconensis	6,000	15
Thracia	4,500	11.5
Pannonia	4,000	10
Gallia Belgica	3,500	9
Syria-Phoenice	2,000	5
Africa-Numidia	2,000	5
Britannia	1,500	4
Syria-Palestina	1,000	2.5
Moesia	1,000	2.5
Gallia Narbonensis	1,000	2.5

Table 1: Cavalry recruitment (after
Hyland 1990: 77)

manpower (Goldsworthy 1998: 29; Le Bohec 2000: 70–73).

The optimum age range was 18 to 23 (Davies 1989: 7), but in Britain the youngest legionary recruits known are Caecilius Donatus and Postumius Solus, who were 14 when they joined up, and the oldest is C. Valerius Victor at 28. Tacitus (*Annales* 4.4) states that Tiberius complained of a shortage of suitable recruits for the army; in Italy only the poorest vagrants were volunteering. The Roman writer Dio (52.27) attributes a speech to Maecenas (poet, friend and adviser to Augustus), in which he counsels the emperor to maintain a strong regular army, since this absorbed men who would otherwise have become bandits. The laws contained in the book *Digesta*, dealing with recruitment, are informative. Men who had been condemned to the wild beasts, deported to an island, exiled for a fixed term not yet expired, were, if discovered in the ranks, to be discharged and punished. The existence of this legislation suggests that such men had been found in the army. It is noticeable that only men guilty of such major crimes were barred, not petty criminals.

Then again, when it comes to the cavalry it appears that things were somewhat better. The evidence suggests that most cavalry recruits were still teenagers or in their early twenties when enlisting and thus, presumably, at the peak of their physical powers. From a range of cavalry tombstones found in Britain it is clear that most troopers started their military service between the ages of 18 and 25.

The benefits

The Roman emperor Severus Alexander is said to have had the motto 'One need not fear a soldier, if he is properly clothed, fully armed, has a stout pair of boots, a full belly, and something in his money-belt' (*SHA* Severus Alexander 52, cf. Vegetius 3.8, Josephus *Bellum Iudaicum* 3.85). Unsurprisingly, military service seems to have been most attractive as a career to the poorest of men. For such men the army offered a roof over their head, food in their bellies, and an annual income in coin. Overall a soldier's life was more secure than that of an itinerant labourer.

Naturally, there was a harsher side to a military career. It came at a price of 25 years of service. During that time a soldier ran the risk of being killed or crippled by battle or disease. On an everyday basis he was subject to the army's brutal discipline, with both corporal and capital punishment being imposed for misdemeanours. The death penalty could be carried out in a number of ways. The most notorious, of course, was the decimation of soldiers found guilty of cowardice in the face of the enemy. Decimation was rarely used, however, and Tacitus describes it as a rare and antiquated penalty (*Annales* 3.21, cf. Suetonius *Divus Augustus* 24.2, Plutarch *Antony* 39.7, Ammianus 24.3.1–2). Promotion was possible, but required a level of education and influence that many soldiers may have lacked. Nor was the legal position of soldiers unambiguously favourable.

Soldiers were forbidden to marry and, to prevent a man's loyalty being split between the army and his family, any marriage contracted prior to service was declared illegal on enlistment. Even so, many men, who were, after all, in the prime of their lives, clearly did develop long-term relationships and began to raise a family during service. Thus the situation changed under Claudius (r.AD 41–54), who, according to the writer Dio (60.24.3), gave soldiers *conubium* (the rights of married men), allowing any unofficial union during service to be made legal on their honourable discharge from the army, and the children to become legitimate. One *decurio* (commander of a *turma*), for instance, T. Claudius Valerius, who died at the age of 50 after 30 years' service with *ala II Hispanorum et Aravacorum*, had his tombstone set up in Teutoburgium, Pannonia, by his wife and daughter (*CIL* III 3271 = Campbell 251).

ORGANIZATION

Cavalry units known as *alae* (wings) are thought to have consisted of 16 *turmae* (Hyginus *De muntionibus castrorum* 16, cf. *CIL* III 6581), each with 30 troopers (Fink 80, cf. Arrian *Tactica* 18.3) commanded by a *decurio* and his second-in-command the *duplicarius*, if they were *quingenaria* (16 × 32 = 512), or if *milliaria* 24 *turmae* (24 × 32 = 768). Drawn from the equestrian order, cavalry commanders were ranked as *praefectus alae* (*ala quingenaria*, *ala milliaria*). These were men who had already served as prefects of auxiliary *cohortes* (*praefectus cohortis*) and either as tribunes in legions (*tribuni angusticlavii*) or tribunes of *cohortes milliariae*. By the mid-2nd century there were some 90 posts as *praefectus alae*, and the commands of the *alae milliariae* devolved on a select group of about ten, consisting of the pick of the men who had already commanded *alae quingenariae*.

Additionally, there were mixed units of infantry and cavalry, the *cohortes equitatae*. Their organization is less clear, but according to the Roman engineer Hyginus (*De muntionibus castrorum* 27), consisted of six centuries of 80 men and four *turmae* of 30 troopers if *cohors equitata quingenaria* (6 × 80 + 4 × 32 = 608); or ten centuries of 80 men and eight *turmae* of 30 troopers if *cohors equitata milliaria* (10 × 80 + 8 × 32 = 1,056). The pride of the Roman cavalry was obviously the horsemen of the *alae*, but more numerous were the horsemen of the *cohortes equitatae*. Having served for some time as infantrymen before being upgraded and trained as cavalrymen, these troopers were not as highly paid, or as well mounted as those of the *alae*, but they performed much of the day-to-day patrolling, policing and escort duties. The *alae* would spend their time in peace on manoeuvres and training, and should hostilities break out they were deployed as a highly mobile strike force, supplemented, if the need arose, by the *cohortes equitatae*. In battle, according to the soldier-scholar Arrian (*fl*.AD 130), the mounted contingents of several cohorts were taken from their parent units and massed to form one composite force, roughly equivalent in size to an *ala* (*Ektaxis* 1–2, 9, cf. *ILS* 2724 with addenda).

Numbers and titles

Like legions, auxiliary units had numbers and names. Those units originally raised in the western provinces generally took their names

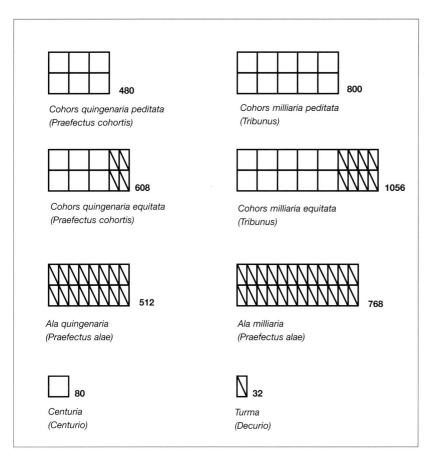

Figure 1: Comparative sizes of auxiliary units (after Keppie 1998: figure 49)

480
Cohors quingenaria peditata
(Praefectus cohortis)

800
Cohors milliaria peditata
(Tribunus)

608
Cohors quingenaria equitata
(Praefectus cohortis)

1056
Cohors milliaria equitata
(Tribunus)

512
Ala quingenaria
(Praefectus alae)

768
Ala milliaria
(Praefectus alae)

80
Centuria
(Centurio)

32
Turma
(Decurio)

from a tribe or region, those in the east from a city. For example, there were five cohorts raised in Gaul, *cohors I–V Gallorum*. Equally, many auxiliary units had titles incorporating the name of an emperor, such as *Augusta, Flavia, Ulpia* or *Aelia.*

Again, like the names of legions, *auxilia* names became interlinked with the unit's history, so emphasizing its distinct identity. *Ala Gallorum et Thracum Classiana invicta bis torquata civium Romanorum* was raised in support of Rome during the Gallic revolt of Tiberius' reign (AD 21). It took the title *Classiana* from the name of its first commander, the Gallic nobleman Classicianus. The later addition of a contingent of Thracians gave it *et Thracum*. It gained the title *invicta* (invincible), and the honour of a torque twice (*bis torquata*), and the premature grant of citizenship to all of its serving men, *civium Romanorum* (of Roman citizens), through its achievements in battle. Henceforth the unit itself employed the designation *c(ivium) R(omanorum)*, but all future recruits remained non-citizens until honourably discharged – citizenship went only to those serving at the moment of the battle honour. The first torque was gained possibly during the reigns of the Flavians (AD 69–96), and the second either during the reign of Trajan (AD 98–117) or that of Hadrian (AD 117–138), on both occasions in Britannia.

Despite their unit titles the *auxilia* recruited locally. For instance, although *ala Gallorum* was initially raised in Gaul, it would have recruited troopers locally once stationed in Britannia and would thus have been made up of Britons by the time it was transferred to Germania Inferior

(AD 122). Regardless of where it was based, the army's word of command and the language of the administration that ran it was Latin. Recruits would have to acquire at least a rudimentary understanding of the language.

Records of auxiliary units show that units were often considerably undermanned, as sickness and the provision of men to assist the civil administration of a province reduced units to around half their paper-strength (Fink 63, 64, *Tab. Vindol.* II 154). These rosters also demonstrate that units might also be divided between several forts, sometimes mixed with troops from other units (*Tab. Vindol.* II 154.5–9), or simply that men were absent from their unit for various reasons (Fink 63.17–40).

Exotics

The arrival of the Roxolani Sarmatians along the Danube in the second half of the 1st century brought Rome face to face with a new type of horsemen. These were *cataphractarii*, first mentioned by Tacitus, heavily armoured horsemen wearing 'iron plating or toughened leather' (*Historiae* 1.79, cf. *Annales* 6.34). Rome's response was, of course, to begin employing these *cataphractarii*. Although some units may have existed earlier, Hadrian formed the first regular unit of *cataphractarii*, *ala I Gallorum et Pannoniorum catafractaria* from Sarmatian settlers in Gaul and Pannonia (*CIL* XI 5632).

Cataphractarii were armed with a heavy spear (Greek *kontōs*, Latin *contus*) some 3.65m (12ft) in length and held two-handed without a shield. It was a weapon for shock action, being driven home with the full thrust of the body behind it. The greater weight of men, horse, and equipment meant their charge was considered to be more powerful

Cataphractarii and *clibanarii*

Ammianus describes the Sassanid Persian method of totally encasing horsemen in metal scale armour, with a helmet in which the 'only spots where a weapon could lodge were the tiny holes left for the eyes and nostrils' (25.1.12). He also says 'their horses were protected by housings of leather' (24.6.8, cf. Heliodorus *Aethiopica* 9.15). These were *clibanarii* ('oven-men' – cf. Greek *klibānos*, baking-oven). By comparison, *cataphractarii* were heavily armoured cavalry: the trooper was an armoured man on a horse that was also usually armoured, but not necessarily so. The Roxolani Sarmatians encountered by the Romans in Moesia (AD 69), for instance, were clad in armour of iron plating or toughened leather. Their horses, however, were not armoured (Tacitus *Historiae* 1.79). Alternatively, Arrian (*Tactica* 4.1) describes *cataphractarii* mounts wearing chamfrons and scale housings.

A description of Roman *clibanarii*, namely those introduced by Constantius II (r.337–361), which accords perfectly with the famous 'charging *clibanarius*' depicted in a third-century graffito at Dura-Europos is given by Ammianus (16.10.8):

And scattered among them were the *cataphractarii equites* (whom they call *clibanarii*), all masked, furnished with protecting breastplates and girt with iron belts, so you might have supposed them statues polished by the hand of Praxiteles, not men. Thin circles of iron plates, fitted to the curves of their bodies, completely covered their limbs; so their garment fitted, so skilfully were the joins made.

The graffito depicts a rider wearing a combination of mail and laminated plate. A short-sleeved mail shirt, such as the complete example found at Dura-Europos (James 2004: 116), was worn in combination with a corselet of overlapping iron plates wrapped around the trunk. The limbs were protected by articulated arm- and leg-guards consisting of overlapping iron plates. Those on the arms overlapped upwards, as required to deflect pointed weapons running up the un-shielded left arm as it gripped the rider's *contus*. Articulated armoured hand-protectors may also have been worn, as they are described by Constantius' successor, Julian (*Orationes* 1.37D).

than that of ordinary cavalry (Tacitus *Historiae* 1.79). As the weight factor prevented *cataphractarii* from charging at anything much faster than a trot, a slow but steady advance by a dense armoured mass meant their shock was more psychological than physical.

At the other end of the scale Rome employed Numidians from Africa. These horsemen, who had wreaked such havoc in the armies of Rome during the war with Hannibal (Polybios 3.72.10, 116.5), were completely un-armoured and rode bareback without even a saddlecloth or a bridle. If a harness was used it was of the simplest type, a rope around the neck and another noosed around the jaw to make a primitive bridle. But sometimes they dispensed even with this, the rider guiding his mount by tapping its neck with the butt of a spear. The weakness of this method was that the rider had no way to enforce his wishes. It might do well enough for skirmishing at a distance, but not for persuading a mount to charge into contact. Yet the Numidians' speed and agility allowed them to charge and withdraw before their opponents could react. Numidians wore a short, sleeveless natural wool tunic and carried a small hide shield without boss, and were armed with a number of light spears. Whilst praising their ability to endure fatigue, Aelian maligns the Numidians as 'slim and dirty like the horses they ride' (*De natura animalium* 3.2, cf. Appian *Bellum Punicum* 11, 71). Likewise Livy (35.11.6–11) describes their horses as small and lean in a passage that praises the Numidians' horsemanship but ridicules their appearance.

BELOW **Italic terracotta plaque showing a Numidian wearing a sheepskin over a tunic. Accustomed to being on horseback from infancy, Numidians rode mounts that looked scrawny and neglected, but were capable of enduring where fleshier animals could not. (Musée du Louvre, Paris; Author's collection)**

Rome also employed horse-archers – the epithet *sagittariorum* in the title of a cavalry unit denoted the men as such – specially drawn from peoples renowned for their skill in this field. Mounted on swift, nimble horses, their prime tactical role was to demoralize and disorganize the enemy by inflicting losses from a distance. Nevertheless, horse-archers were probably equipped with shafted weapons as well as the formidable composite bow. The composite bow combined layers of sinew, wood and horn to create a weapon with a balance of strength under tensile and compressive forces that enabled an efficient transfer of the potential energy stored in the fully drawn bow. Its design took full advantage of the mechanical properties of the materials used in its construction. Sinew has great tensile strength, while horn has compressive strength. When released, the horn belly acts like a coil, returning instantly to its original position. Sinew, on the other hand, naturally contracts after being stretched, which is exactly what happens to the convex back of the bow as it snaps back to resume its original shape. This method of construction and the materials employed thus allow the bow to impart a greater degree of force to the arrow when fired, compared with the wooden self-bow of the same draw weight.

EQUIPMENT AND APPEARANCE

As with all professional, state-sponsored armies, improvements in equipment took place relatively slowly, necessitating the continued use of material that was of considerable age, even if certain older items, helmets in particular, were relegated to inferior grades of soldier. It may be said with truth of Roman military equipment that as long as a piece remained in serviceable condition, it continued to be used. Much Roman military equipment retains traces of its ethnic origins, so it comes as no great surprise to find that the equestrian arms and equipment were largely based on Celtic originals.

Helmet
Roman helmets, which were influenced by Celtic styles, were made of iron or copper alloy (both bronze and brass are known). The main features are the skull-shaped bowl, a large nape-guard at right angles to the head to deflect blows to the neck, and large cheek-guards to protect the sides of the face.

The helmet invariably left the face and ears exposed, since the soldier needed to see and hear to understand and follow battlefield commands. Unlike infantry helmets, however, cavalry helmets covered the ears, the extra protection to the face clearly considered to be more important than some loss of hearing. Also the nape-guard was very deep, reaching down to close to the shoulders, but it was not wide, since this would have made the rider likely to break his neck if he fell from his horse. The cavalry helmet, therefore, protected equally well against blows to the side and the back of the head, vital in a cavalry mêlée when the two sides soon become intermingled.

By the turn of the 2nd century the crown of the helmet was reinforced with cross braces secured with conical rivets, while a brow-guard, which defended against downward blows to the

Bronze facemask from Newstead–*Trimontium*. This example, probably from a sports helmet, has strong feminine characteristics and may represent an Amazon, one of a race of female warriors alleged to have existed in Scythia. (Museum of Scotland, Edinburgh; photograph Esther Carré)

face, was applied to the forehead (auxiliary cavalry type 'E'). Over time, this gradually rose more and more at the front, eventually forming a pointed peak.

Boots

Military boots, or *caligae*, were made from ox-hide and cut out from a one-piece upper, sewn up at the heel, and had separate 20mm-thick soles finished with conical iron hobnails. Weighing a little under a kilogram, the boots were laced all the way up the front. The nailing designs on the sole were arranged very ergonomically and anticipate modern training-shoe soles designed to optimize the transferral of weight between the different parts of the foot when placed on the ground. Sculptural evidence, such as the Cancellaria relief, shows that *undones* (woollen socks), open at the toe and the heel, could be worn within the boot.

Cavalrymen could attach iron or bronze spurs to their *caligae*. Prick spurs had been worn by Celts of the La Tène period, being evident in early Iron Age Gallic and central European graves and settlements, and were known in Greece from the late 5th century BC onwards (Xenophon *Peri Hippikis* 8.5, 10.2, Pollux 10.53–54). They were sporadically used by Roman cavalry throughout the empire, especially by troopers on the Rhine-Danube frontier.

Body armour

The Romans employed three main types of body armour: *lorica hamata* (mail), *lorica squamata* (scale), and *lorica segmentata* (segmented, a term coined during the Renaissance). The latter type was worn by legionaries only.

All body armour would have been worn over some kind of padded garment, not directly on top of the tunic. Apart from making the wearer more comfortable, this extra layer complemented the protective values of each type of armour, and helped to absorb the shock of any blow striking the armour. The anonymous author of the *De rebus bellicis*, an amateur military theoretician writing in the late 4th century, describes the virtues of such a garment: 'The ancients [i.e. the Romans], among the many things, which … they devised for use in war, prescribed also the *thoracomachus* to counteract the weight and friction of armour … This type of garment is made of thick sheep's wool felt to the measure … of the upper part of the human frame …' (15.1–2). The author himself probably coined the term *thoracomachus* (cf. Greek *thorāx*, breastplate), which seems to be a padded garment of linen stuffed with wool. One scene on Trajan's Column (CXXVIII) depicts two dismounted troopers on sentry duty outside a headquarters who appear to have removed their mail-shirts to expose the padded garment.

Mail was normally made of iron rings, on average about 1mm thick and 3–9mm in external diameter. Each ring was connected to four others, each one passing through the two rings directly above and two directly below – one riveted ring being inter-linked with four punched rings. In the early Principate the wearer's shoulders were reinforced

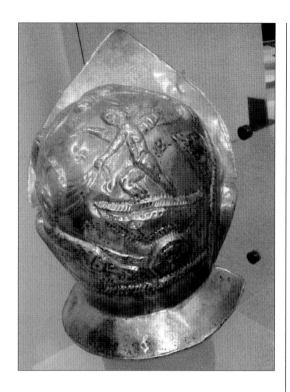

Brass helmet of cavalry sports type 'B' from Newstead–*Trimontium*. Manufactured during the second half of the 1st century, the skull piece is decorated with a winged Cupid riding a chariot pulled by two leopards. (Museum of Scotland, Edinburgh; photograph Esther Carré)

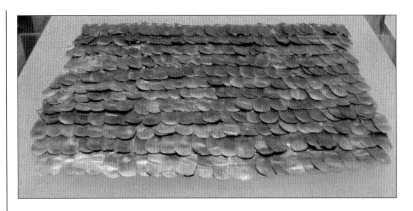

Bronze scales from Newstead–*Trimontium*. Each scale has four side-link holes and one lacing hole at the top. This piece dates to the end of the 1st century and probably belonged to a cavalryman stationed at the fort. (Museum of Scotland, Edinburgh; photograph Esther Carré)

with 'doubling', of which there were two types. One had comparatively narrow shoulder 'straps', and a second pattern, probably derived from earlier Celtic patterns, in the form of a shoulder-cape. The second type required no backing leather, being simply drawn around the wearer's shoulder girdle and fastened with S-shaped breast-hooks, which allowed the shoulder-cape to move more easily. The shoulder-cape is indicated on numerous grave markers belonging to cavalrymen, which also show the mail-shirt split at the hips to enable the rider to sit on a horse.

Although mail had two very considerable drawbacks – it was extremely laborious to make and was very heavy at 10–15kg (22–33lb) – it nevertheless afforded complete freedom of movement to the wearer and was popular. A mail-shirt was flexible and essentially shapeless, fitting more closely to the wearer's body than other types of armour. In this respect it was comfortable, whilst the wearing of a belt helped to spread its considerable weight, which would otherwise be carried entirely by the shoulders. Mail offered reasonable protection, but could be penetrated by a strong thrust or an arrow fired at effective range.

Scale armour was made of small plates 1–5cm ($\frac{1}{2}$–2in) in length, of copper alloy, or occasionally of iron, wired to their neighbours horizontally and then sewn in overlapping rows to linen or leather backing. Each row was arranged to overlap the one below by a third to a half the height of the scales, enough to cover the vulnerable stitching. The scales themselves were thin, and the main strength of this protection came from the overlap of scale to scale, which helped to spread the force of a blow.

A serious deficiency lay in the fact that such defences could be quite readily pierced by an upward thrust of sword or spear, a hazard that many cavalrymen must have been acutely aware of when engaging infantry. This weakness was overcome, certainly by the 2nd century, when a new form of semi-rigid cuirass was introduced where each scale, of a relatively large dimension, was wired to its vertical, as well as its horizontal, neighbours.

Scale could be made by virtually anyone, requiring patience rather than craftsmanship, and was very simple to repair. Though scale was far inferior to mail, being neither as strong nor as flexible, it was similarly used throughout the Principate and proved particularly popular with troopers as this type of armour, especially if tinned, could be polished to a high sheen.

Shields

Cavalrymen carried *clipeus* (flat shields), either oval or hexagonal in shape. To be light enough to be held continually in battle, shield-boards were usually constructed of double or triple thickness plywood made up of thin strips of birch or plane wood held together with glue. The middle layer was laid at right angles to the front and back layers.

Trajan's Column (scene XLII): the emperor delivers a speech (*adlocutio*) to members of his army, including auxiliary cavalrymen. Though the auxiliaries, infantry and cavalry alike carry the flat, oval *clipeus*, the artist has depicted a variety of shield designs. (Reproduced from Lepper-Frere XXXIII)

Covered both sides with linen and rawhide, they were edged with copper-alloy binding and had a central iron or copper-alloy boss (*umbo*) covering a horizontal handgrip and wide enough to clear the fist of the bearer.

When not in use the shield was carried obliquely against the horse's flank (Josephus *Bellum Iudaicum* 3.96), hung from the two side-horns of the saddle and sometimes under the saddlecloth (Trajan's Column scenes V, XLII, XLIX, LXXXIX, CIV). It was protected by a leather shield-cover, which was tightened round the rim of the shield by a drawstring.

Spears

Cavalry used a *lancea* (light spear) approximately 1.8m (6ft) long. It was suitable for throwing or thrusting over-arm as shown in the figured tombstones of the period. Even though such funerary carvings usually depict troopers either carrying two *lancae*, or *calones* (grooms) behind them holding spares, Josephus (*Bellum Iudaicum* 3.96) claims that Vespasian's eastern cavalry carried a quiver containing three or more darts with points as large as light spears. He did not say specifically where the quiver was positioned, but presumably it was attached to the saddle. Arrian (*Tactica* 40.10–11) confirms this in his description of the cavalry exercises in which horsemen were expected to throw as many as 15, or, in exceptional cases 20 light spears, in one run. Analysis

Selection of Roman iron spearheads from Newstead–*Trimontium* with tubular shanks and sockets to permit riveting to shafts. Carried by cavalrymen, *lancae* were fairly light, and could be thrown or kept in hand for close-quarter combat. (Museum of Scotland, Edinburgh; photograph Esther Carré)

of the remains of wooden shafts shows that ash and hazel were commonly used.

Swords

Cavalry used a *spatha* (a long, narrow, double-edged broadsword), with a blade length from 64.5–91.5cm (25–36in) and width from 4–6cm (1½–2½in). The middle section of the blade was virtually parallel-edged, but tapered into a rounded point. It was intended primarily as a slashing weapon for use on horseback, though the point could also be used.

The *spatha* was worn on the right side of the body, as numerous cavalry tombstones show, suspended from a waist belt or baldric whose length could be adjusted by a row of metal buttons. From the 2nd century onwards, however, the *spatha* started to be worn on the left side, although not exclusively so.

Standards

The standard, or *vexillum*, was a square pierce of red or purple material with fringing on the bottom edge, which hung from a crossbar attached to the upper part of a wooden pole. *Vexillarii*, the men who carried this standard, are recorded for the *alae* (*ILS* 9190) in addition to being depicted on Trajan's Column (scenes VII, LXXXIX).

Another type of standard attested for the *alae* is the *imago*, which bore the image of the emperor. The office of *imaginifer*, the bearer of this standard, is recorded on an inscription (*AE* 1906.119). Obviously standards played an important function in the Roman army, for not only were they a rallying point for troops and a method of relaying signals in battle, but they also had a cultic significance.

Horses

The size of a horse does not have a great bearing on its ability to carry weight, but its build does, and this also affects its length of service (Hyland 1990: 67). As a grazing animal, it relies on speed to outstrip predators, but speed is not a major requirement for a warhorse. Any *ala*

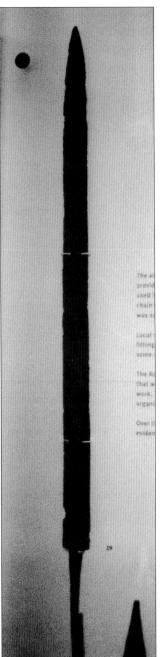

LEFT Dismounted *vexillarii* on Trajan's Column (scene VII) each carrying a *vexillum*, a square flag hung from a crossbar and almost certainly embroidered with a design. Standards were physical expressions of a unit's corporate identity and were treated with reverence. (Reproduced from Lepper-Frere IX)

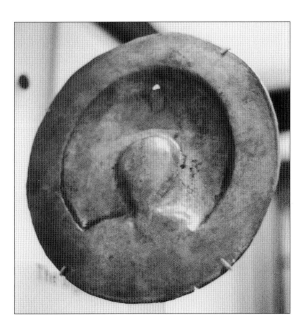

would travel at a conservative speed – cavalry travelling alone could average 50–65km (30–40 miles) a day without overtaxing the animals – except when harrying or in a sudden charge. The more compact the animal, the greater its load-bearing capacity, and the short stocky breeds that still retain enough refinement to give a smooth ride and achieve sufficient speed are far more suited to warfare than overlarge, lumbering, excessively heavy-fleshed animals. Ann Hyland (1990: 154), an experienced equestrian and experimental archaeologist, estimates that a Roman cavalry horse carried a total weight of some 104kg (229lb).

A horse's height is measured from a point just in front of the saddle, specifically at the withers, the unit of measurement being a hand of 4 inches (10cm). The analysis of the osteological remains belonging to nine Roman cavalry mounts found at Newstead–*Trimontium*, Scotland, show that in life these were between 11.2 and 14 hands (Curle 1911: 362–371). The smaller horses were of the 'Celtic' variety, very similar to a modern Welsh Mountain Pony, and it is not entirely out of the question that cavalrymen rode these small animals. The Romans had also imported other varieties similar to the slender-limbed modern Arab, perhaps from Gaul, and also slightly larger Libyans. Of the latter breed, Aelian commented that they 'are exceedingly swift and know little or nothing of fatigue' (*De natura animalium* 3.2); this is corroborated by Strabo (17.3.7), who added that they were small and obedient. There were also two different types of crossbreeds, imported perhaps from Germania. Other evidence comes from the archaeological site of Krefeld-Gellep, Germany, where many Roman horses were found over an extended period of excavation. Of the 31 horses unearthed, all dated to sometime in the 1st century, only two were of 11.2 and 12.2 hands. The rest varied from 13.2 to 15.1 hands (Nobis 1973: 251).

Varro states in *De re rustica* (2.7.15) that the Romans quite commonly employed mares – a view confirmed by Pliny the Elder (*Naturalis historia* 8.42) when he notes that mares were preferred for military uses. Among the papyri found at Dura-Europos (a Syro-Mesopotamian city on the middle Euphrates annexed by Rome in AD 165 and garrisoned by its auxiliaries) was a 'horse list' from the records of *cohors XX Palmyrenorum milliaria equitata* (Fink 83). Dating to AD 251, it catalogues 13 horses, only three of which are mares (lines 4, 8, 19), two not specified, and the rest males (presumably stallions). Of the 31 horses found at Krefeld-Gellep, however, around half were male and half female.

Four-horned saddle

The saddle became part of Roman cavalry equipment from at least the time of C. Iulius Caesar, a concession, so he says (*Bellum Gallicum* 4.4.2), considered effete by the Germans. The padded saddle with four horns (*cornicule*), made by internal bronze stiffeners, appears for the first time on Roman sculptures (Arc d'Orange, Mausoleum at Saint-Rémy-de-Provence) of the early Principate. Like most equestrian equipment, it was almost certainly of Celtic origin as it is depicted on the Gundestrup cauldron[1] (which probably pre-dates the 1st century BC).

When a rider's weight was lowered onto this type of saddle the four tall horns closed around and gripped his thighs, but they did not inhibit free movement to the same extent as a modern pommel and cantle designed for rider comfort and safety. This was especially important to spear-armed horsemen, whose drill called for some acrobatic changes of position. In an age that did not have the stirrup, the adoption of the four-horned saddle allowed the horseman to launch a missile effectively while skirmishing, or use both hands confidently to wield his shield and spear (or sword) in a whirling mêlée (Hyland 1990: 130–134, 1993: 45–51).

The main function of its wooden frame was to protect the horse's spine from shock during a charge, and its design transferred the rider's weight to the animal's flanks. The saddle was secured with breast strap, haunch straps and breeching, and a girth that passed through a woollen saddlecloth under which a smaller cloth of fur may have been placed to give the horse greater protection from chafing. A number of sculptural examples show cloths that cover the horse's flanks and terminate in tassels or fringes (Trajan's Column scenes XXXVIII, XLII, LVII, LVIII, CXLII, CXLV), while other examples depict a combination of a small saddlecloth over a larger one with a fringed border (Trajan's Column scenes XXIV, XXXVI, XXXVII, XLIX, LXXXIX).

Horse furniture

The leather harness-straps and bridle were decorated with non-functional brass pendants and linked with *phalerae* (disc-junctions) made of niello-inlaid, silvered or tinned bronze. These are also of Celtic origin and appear, for example, on the Gundestrup cauldron.

The horns of a Roman saddle were reinforced with copper-alloy plates and then padded and covered in leather. These are from Newstead–*Trimontium*. The left plate stiffened a rear horn, that on the right a front one. (Museum of Scotland, Edinburgh; photograph Esther Carré)

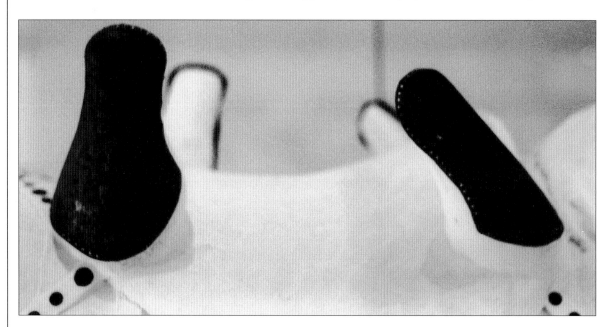

[1] The silver Gundestrup cauldron, probably a votive offering, was discovered in a peat bog in Denmark. From the late Bronze Age onwards cauldrons were used as sacred vessels. Strabo describes how a prisoner-of-war could be sacrificed by having his throat cut over a cauldron, and cauldrons have also been found as water offerings both inside and outside the Celtic world. If not actually Celtic, the Gundestrup cauldron is heavily influenced by La Tène art and life.

Sometimes the horse wore a decorative fringed *peytral* (chest band) of soft leather.

There were two main classes of bit in use. One type was a snaffle bit of Celtic inspiration, with two free-moving rings to hold the reins and harness, which acted primarily on the tongue and the bars of the mouth. The other type was an Italic curb bit with a tongued bar that went in the mouth, and a chain or straight bar that went under the chin of the horse, making it much more responsive to the reins, especially when the rider was using only one hand.

The Romans also employed hackamores in conjunction with bits. These were metal 'muzzles', which consisted of a bar that ran above the

Dismounted cavalrymen on Trajan's Column (scene XLIX) pass a Roman fortification. The horse harness and four-horned saddle are evident on the lead horse, as well as the shield suspended from the saddle and covered by the smaller of two saddlecloths. (Reproduced from Lepper-Frere XXXVI)

Dismounted troopers on Trajan's Column (scene V) leading their horses off a pontoon bridge spanning the Danube. A combination of a small saddlecloth over a larger one is clearly seen on the horse in the forefront of this scene. (Reproduced from Lepper-Frere VIII)

nose and under the chin of the horse. They were attached by rings and eyes to the bridle straps and the reins, and prevented the horse from opening its mouth and 'getting away' from the bit.

Horse armour

Two intact horse-bards for *cataphractarii* were found at Dura-Europos: Housing I had copper-alloy scales and measured 1.22m by 1.69m wide (4ft long by 5ft 6in); Housing II was iron, measured 1.48m by 1.1m wide (4ft 10in long by 3ft 7in), and differed slightly with extensions at the front that went round the horse's breast. Dated to the mid-3rd century, they would fit a stocky horse between 15 and 15.3 hands high, laying over its back much like a modern horse blanket. Both pieces are of overlapping metal scales sewn on to a doubled backing of coarse linen, with a wide strip of leather along the spine probably to prevent chafing. A hole had been cut in the barding to allow it to fit over the saddle, and all edges were finished in red-dyed leather. Both bards have a tail guard, roughly triangular in shape, attached to protect the dock (James 2004: 129–132).

Roman horse harnesses were decorated with tinned or silvered *phalerae* and pendants. These are seen here on a funerary relief of an unknown cavalryman (the inscription is missing). Note the tall horns of the saddle. (Author's collection)

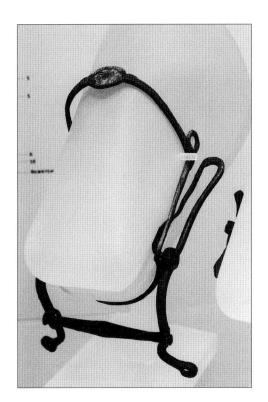

Armour of this type could also be made of horn scales, lacquered rawhide scales, or of thick felt. Judging from the depictions of captured Sarmatian arms and armour on the base (south-west face) of Trajan's Column, it seems the Sarmatians favoured the first of these. Horse armour for *cataphractarii* would have also included a protective head covering, or chamfron (Arrian *Tactica* 4.1), and neck armour, as shown in a graffito from Dura-Europos.

A horse-bard had definite advantages, even if it had serious drawbacks such as restricting the mobility and speed of the horse. It offered some protection against cutting and thrusting weapons, and against almost spent arrows. The scales could turn a blade, forcing it to glissade off, or at best deliver a more glancing blow. However, if the thrust was powerful enough or the arrow's force in flight not spent, the scales could be driven into the animal's flesh, causing a nasty wound. An arrow, particularly from a composite bow, would lodge deep into the armour, or carry some of it into the horse's flesh. According to Dio (36.5.1–2), a Parthian arrow was especially vicious: they were delivered by a composite bow and carried double barbs designed to break off inside the victim's flesh. One of the Dura-Europos bards (Housing III) has a hole in it, apparently caused by a *ballista* missile (James 2004: 133).

ABOVE **This iron curb bit from Newstead–*Trimontium* is especially severe. The slightest one-handed tug on the reins would ensure instant obedience from the horse, a necessary requirement for any cavalryman in the heat of battle. (Museum of Scotland, Edinburgh; photograph Esther Carré)**

TRAINING AND EXERCISES

'Their battle-drills are no different from the real thing … it would not be far from the truth to call their drills bloodless battles, their battles

RIGHT **Fleeing Sarmatian *cataphractarii* on Trajan's Column (scene XXXVII). The depiction of scales fitting closely against the horses' hooves probably results from hearsay, as extant examples of horse bardings fall vertically down the flank of the animal. (Reproduced from Lepper-Frere XXVIII)**

The chamfron from Newstead–*Trimontium* comprises a leather mask with circular eyeholes, prominent earflaps, and an overall design executed in metal studs. Stitching holes indicate that a nameplate once sat just below the eyeholes. (Museum of Scotland, Edinburgh; photograph Esther Carré)

bloody drills'. So wrote Josephus (*Bellum Iudaicum* 3.76), who presents an idealized view of the army's efficiency. But while warriors of many different peoples were well practised in the use of their personal weapons, only the Romans trained both as individuals and units. In his etymological studies Varro reverses what we would consider to be the normal order of things when he says '*exercitus quod exercitando fit melior*' (*De lingua Latina* 5.87, cf. Cicero *Tusculanae Disputationes* 2.16.37) – 'An army performs better if it is trained.' In other words, he derives the term for 'army' (*exercitus*) from the verb 'to exercise' (*exercitare*). It is training, both individual and collective, that largely explains the success of the Roman army.

Without a doubt the most valuable and instructive source on cavalry training is Arrian's *Ars Tactica* (*Téchne Takitké*), which was composed in AD 136 on the direct instructions of Hadrian, himself a noted hunter and horseman. The second part of it deals specifically with the Roman cavalry. Similarly, though his two equestrian treatises, *Art of Horsemanship* (*Peri Hippikis*) and *Cavalry Commander* (*Hipparchikos*), concern the horsemen of ancient Athens, the soldier-scholar Xenophon (*c.*428–355 BC) also provides excellent details about horses, riding and the organization and command of cavalry. It is appropriate to cite a Greek writer, especially one who was such an authority on horsemanship, as the only real difference between the training of cavalry would be the language used to instruct the horse. A Roman commander of Greek origin, Arrian (*c.*AD 97–175) also studied Xenophon very closely when he compiled his *Tactica*, and even adopted the *nom de plume* of Xenophon in his technical works.

Training the man

Many troopers in the *alae* were already proficient at riding and fighting after their native fashions before they were enlisted into the Roman army. Later, as a unit retained its name, its gradually lost its ethnic content, and relied on individual or small-batch recruitment to retain its strength. Newly recruited cavalrymen had to be trained to ride, and some had to be taught from scratch, especially newly promoted horsemen of the *cohortes equitata*. Vegetius (1.18) makes this clear when he explains that troopers first tried mounting from either side on wooden horses without accoutrements, and later progressed to mounting when fully armed.

Gradually recruits progressed to the real thing, and here the first step would be how to sit on a horse correctly. An expert horseman himself, Xenophon provided the basic instructions:

> The lower leg including the foot must hang lax and easy from the knee down ... The rider must also accustom himself to keeping the body above the hips as loose as possible, for thus he will be able to stand more fatigue and will be less liable to come off when he is pulled or pushed. (*Peri Hippikis* 7.6–7.)

As Hyland says, this 'position enabled the rider to move with his horse, feel the horse's back muscle movements and be forewarned of the horse's next move' (2003: 42).

With such basics mastered, the recruit would then proceed to tuition on the use of weapons on horseback and the equestrian manoeuvres used within the cavalry. Initially this may have been performed on the wooden horse, but at the finish he was expected to be able to mount armoured, armed, and with the *spatha* drawn if necessary while the horse was moving. Arrian (*Tactica* 43.3–4) shows that such proficiency was not new in his day.

Although cavalry training required the presence of particularly competent riding and drill instructors, the *exercitator* and the *magister campi*, Vegetius lists among the duties of a *decurio*, the *turma* commander, the following responsibilities: 'He must teach the men in his *turma* every aspect of cavalry fighting ... both cavalryman and horse must be worked continually. Accordingly, the *decurio* is responsible for the health and exercising of both trooper and mount' (2.14). Vegetius also says (1.27) the cavalry trained, fully armed and divided into their *turmae*, on 20-mile (32-kilometre) marches three times a month. During the trek they practised, obviously under the watchful eyes of the *decuriones*, their equestrian evolutions, pursuing, retreating, counter-charging, all to be conducted on varied terrain so horses could work in both flat and rough country. The role of the horse was equal to the role of the man.

Training the horse
Clearly the training of both horse and rider should be carried out simultaneously, but before the new cavalry mount was assigned to the new recruit the two would have undergone some separate basic training already. Xenophon, who throughout the *Peri Hippikis* has an eye to the horse's use in battle, provides the most detailed description of the points to look for in selecting and purchasing a mount for use as a warhorse. Understandably he advises the reader to thoroughly scrutinize the horse before it is purchased and trained as a cavalry remount. This examination should also test the horse's strength and ability in various strenuous exercises that war would bring, 'namely leaping over ditches, jumping over walls, rushing up and springing off banks, and also galloping up and down hills and on the slope' (*Peri Hippikis* 3.7, cf.

Arrian *Tactica* 44.2). He then gives a brief description of the type of horse required for military use:

> To sum up: the horse that is sound-footed, gentle, fairly speedy, has the will and the stamina to stand up to hard work, and above all, is obedient, is the horse that will, as is to be expected, give the least trouble and the greatest measure of safety to his rider in battle. Conversely, a mount that requires a lot of driving on account of his sluggishness, or much coaxing and attention, because of its high spirit, makes constant demands on the rider's hands and robs him of confidence in moments of danger. (*Peri Hippikis* 3.12)

The scrutiny of a horse, therefore, will have consisted of a detailed veterinary examination – checking, amongst other things, the teeth – and careful attention was also paid to the spirit of the animal.

The provision of remounts for the Roman army seems to have been supervised by the provincial government, and it is likely that the responsibility for all military horses rested with the governor himself. One of his duties was to prevent the removal from his province of any *equum militarem* (military horse), as attested by a law (*Digesta* 49.16.12) that dates originally from the 2nd century. Naturally, the governor did not personally perform the scrutiny of horses. The veterinary examination alone would require specialist knowledge, and this task was probably undertaken by imperial officials known as *stratores* (*ILS* 2418, *RIB* 233, Ammianus 29.3.5).

Having passed its examination, or *probatio* (the terms used to describe both men and horses were the same), the equine recruit would then be trained for military service. In his *Georgics* the Augustan poet Virgil gives some information on basic procedure. He recommends schooling a three-year-old horse 'to pace the ring [*gyrus*], to tread the ground with regular-sounding footsteps, and to trace alternate circles with his lissom legs' (3.191–193). Varro (*De re rustica* 2.7.13) and Columella (*De re rustica* 6.29.4) likewise recommend that breaking a horse should not commence until it is three years old. At this stage, as Virgil makes clear, a rider did not take any part in training the horse. All the instruction is in the hands of an experienced trainer, who controls the horse on a set of long-reins, where he is made to trot in circles in both directions, learning obedience to the trainer's voice. Virgil (*Georgics* 3.200–207) makes it fairly obvious that it is no easy thing to bend a horse to man's will, but makes no distinction between either cavalry or racehorses.

From other authorities, however, it is possible to piece together a brief outline of military schooling undertaken once the horse was used to carrying the weight of a man. By now the rider would take control, directing the horse by rein and leg movements. Battle dictates the need for quick turns, levades, sudden stops, and equally sudden spurts, half- and quarter-turns, and in his manual Arrian describes in detail several manoeuvres required of horses, done at various speeds but mostly at the gallop, such as wheeling, turning, and moving in a straight line and at an angle.

Tacitus says (*Germania* 6.3) that Roman horses were trained to execute various turns, unlike German mounts. Arrian (*Tactica*

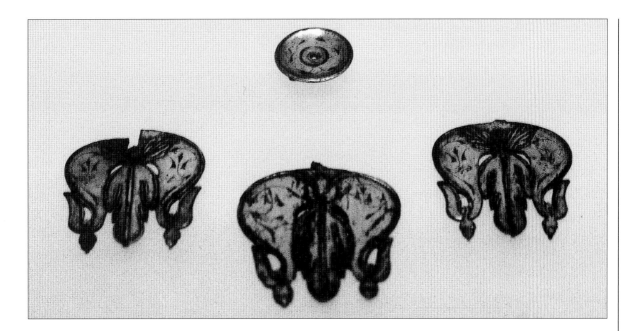

44.1) confirms that Hadrian instructed the Roman cavalry to learn the half- and quarter-turns used by Sarmatian and Celtic horsemen. From the latter a number of equestrian and missile handling manoeuvres were also adopted, such as the *petrinos* (*Tactica* 37.4–5), the *xynema* (*Tactica* 42.1) and the *touloutegon* (*Tactica* 43.2–3). Actually, Arrian (*Tactica* 33.1) acknowledges that, by the time of Hadrian, most of the commands given in cavalry exercises were Celtic in origin and this does support the notion of a strong Gallic element in Roman horsemanship under the Principate. He also says that the horse was taught to stand still while the rider mounted it 'using all the various methods and styles there are' (*Tactica* 43.3, cf. Xenophon *Peri Hippikis* 7.8). A final point comes from Vegetius, who says (1.10, cf. 2.23, 3.4) that horses were to be trained and exercised in swimming both in sea and river water.

Silvered-bronze harness fittings from Newstead–*Trimontium*. In front are trefoil pendants, non-functional decorative pieces that hung from disc-junctions (*phalerae*). The *phalerae* (one example is at the rear), were backed with loops through which the leather harness-straps were passed. (Museum of Scotland, Edinburgh; photograph Esther Carré)

Training exercises

In the final stage of training, sword and spear work would begin, as well as cross-country riding to accustom both horse and rider to the tasks they would be expected to perform as part of normal duties. Xenophon recommends that:

> It is a good method of training for two riders to work together thus: one flies on his horse over all kinds of ground and retreats, reversing his spear so that it points backwards, while the other pursues, having buttons on his javelins and holding his spear in the same position, and when he gets within javelin shot, tries to hit the fugitive with the blunted weapons, and if he gets near enough to use his spear, strike his captive with it. (*Peri Hippikis* 8.10)

One of the best methods of training cavalry and improving their skills is by displays and tournaments. Xenophon (*Hipparchikos* 3.1–14, cf. 1.20) fully appreciates this fact and advocates the same practice for the horsemen of Athens (Fields 2003A: 116–117).

The Roman cavalry was no exception to this rule. Using special training- and practice-weapons, the cavalry practised a complex series of drills involving movement in formation and the throwing of missiles, culminating in the spectacular *hippika gymnasia*, or cavalry games, which took place on the *campus* (parade ground) situated outside every auxiliary fort. Arrian (*Tactica* 34–44) provides a comprehensive description of the *hippika gymnasia* in which two opposed cavalry units performed, no doubt watched by senior officers and honoured guests. One of the units made a charge, and the other tried to hit them with dummy javelins, 'made without iron', while at the same time defending themselves against the general assault. The two units took turns at charging and defending, just as they would in actual combat, demonstrating that the most important attribute of a cavalryman was to be able to throw his weapons fast and accurately while at full gallop and simultaneously defending himself against enemy attacks.

A commemorative monument from Lambaesis, Numidia, records a speech, or *adlocutio* delivered by Hadrian in the summer of AD 128 to the provincial garrison after it had undergone several days of exercises (*ILS* 2487, 9133–9135 = Campbell 17). When addressing the cavalry contingent of *cohors VI Commagenorum equitata*, he commented that it was difficult for such a unit to perform satisfactorily immediately after *ala I Pannoniorum*, with its larger numbers, better equipment and mounts, had put on a display, before expressing his praise for their achievement. Occasionally, the emperor expressed disapproval of a drill, for instance criticising a cavalry unit for mounting a charge that was too fast and uncontrolled, but his speech is an overwhelming one of praise for the units and especially their officers.

A decade earlier Soranus, a trooper of *cohors III Batavorum milliaria equitata*, had performed on manoeuvres in front of Hadrian, in what he claims in his epitaph was a unique feat (*ILS* 2558 = Campbell 47). After swimming the Danube in full battle kit, he shot an arrow in the air and hit it with a second one before the first fell to earth. The unit was not bow-armed (*sagittaria*) and Soranus displayed a skill of little practical use in battle, but he did this, as Dio confirms (69.9.6), on manoeuvres. In fact, the Batavians were famous for their prowess at swimming, and most of them were organized in *cohortes equitatae*. Tacitus says (*Historiae* 4.12, cf. *Agricola* 18.4) that their horsemen could swim rivers while keeping hold of their arms and mounts and maintaining perfect formation.

It seems that during the reign of Hadrian at least, the cavalry were constantly being put through their paces. Arrian, as the new governor of Cappadocia, made an extensive tour of his territory in AD 131 and inspected the various military installations and units under his command. At Hyssus he watched 20 troopers throwing their *lancae*, and at Sebastopolis inspected the troopers of an *ala*, along with their weapons and exercises (Arrian *Periplus maris Euxini* 3.1, 10.3). Detailed instructions in the method of throwing training- and practice-weapons were given in such military manuals as that compiled by Pliny the Elder in a treatise entitled *Javelin-throwing from Horseback* (*de Iaculatione Equestri*, Pliny *Epistulae* 3.5). Sadly this work is lost to us, but in his *Peri Hippikis* Xenophon recommends the rider, for greater impetus and range, to 'advance his left side, draw back his right, rise from his thighs and let the javelin go with the point slightly raised' (12.13).

Iron sports helmet from Newstead–*Trimontium.* This example is almost complete, and represents a youth with an elaborate hairstyle. The tubes and rings held plumes and streamers; the latter were commonly yellow, according to Arrian. (Museum of Scotland, Edinburgh; photograph Esther Carré)

CONDITIONS OF SERVICE

In spite of the rigours of Roman military training and the notorious severity of its discipline, Roman soldiers were very far from being unquestionably obedient in the way expected of soldiers in more recent times. The generally high levels of military effectiveness that they sustained over so many generations are attributed to motivation and *ésprit de corps* as much as to training and discipline. For it is evident that in both peace and war, their commanders, from the emperor down, had to exhort and persuade soldiers to their duty, to pander to their sentiments and prejudices, as much as to regulate, command and coerce them. Not surprisingly, remuneration, booty and victuals each played an important part.

Pay

Annual pay for an *eques* (trooper) serving in an *ala* was 1,050 *sestertii* (262.5 *denarii*), rising to 1,400 *sestertii* (350 *denarii*) under Domitian (r.AD 81–96).[2] A trooper of a *cohors equitata* received the same pay as a

---

[2] Sesterii were bronze coins, four of which were equivalent to one silver denarius.

legionary: under Augustus the annual rate of pay for a legionary was fixed at 900 *sestertii* (225 *denarii*, compared with the 187.5 *denarii* of auxiliary infantryman), rising to 1,200 (300 *denarii*) under Domitian (Tacitus *Annales* 1.17.6, Suetonius *Domitian* 7.5, 12.1). The army stuck to one basic principle – namely, pay was linked to status. Hence some men, including the *principales* and those in other junior posts, received pay-and-a-half (*sesquiplicarii*) or double pay (*duplicarii*).

Before Domitian, wages were paid in three annual instalments, or *stipendia*. His pay-rise perhaps added a fourth instalment. The first payment was made on the occasion of the annual New Year parade when the troops renewed their oath to the emperor. Official deductions were made for food (*ad victum*) and fodder (*capitum*) (Fink 68). In addition, each soldier had to pay for his own clothing, equipment and weapons, but these items were purchased back by the army from the soldier or his heir when he retired or died. For cavalrymen, besides the extra expense of purchasing fodder, the horse was probably regarded as part of the trooper's equipment. Third-century papyri from Dura-Europos indicate 125 *denarii* as the standard amount charged to troopers for their mounts (Fink 83, 99, cf. 75). This figure was presumably set by the military authorities and was not the actual market value of the animal.

Rewards

Arrian (*Tactica* 38.4–5, 40.10–12, 42.5) recommended that troopers who gave a good performance in their exercises should receive praise, just as

The entrance and stairs to the subterranean strong room in the *principia*, Chesters–*Cilurnum* cavalry fort. This small vaulted cellar would have housed the troopers' savings. An ironbound oaken door was found at the entrance, but disintegrated shortly after being exposed. (Author's collection)

those who gave a bad one should be censured. Hadrian, however, believed that soldiers who gave a first-rate performance when on manoeuvres should receive financial as well as verbal commendation (*SHA* Hadrian 10.2). Indeed donatives – irregular cash disbursements in the name of the emperor – became an important supplement to pay. Under the Republic donatives were granted to celebrate the end of a campaign, or to individuals for acts of valour. Yet warlords like C. Iulius Caesar used these cash handouts to instil personal loyalty among their troops, and it soon became the practice for an emperor to distribute donatives on politically sensitive occasions.

For the republican soldier, loot and booty were at the heart of his pay. Although the reward system persisted under the Principate, and soldiers could still make sizeable profits, there was a growing recognition of the need for a definite system that would reward years of service and rank, as well as exceptional individual acts (Tacitus *Historiae* 1.51, 3.33, Josephus *Bellum Iudaicum* 6.317). After the sack of Jerusalem in AD 70, for instance, Titus, the eldest son of Vespasian (r.AD 69–79) and future emperor, rewarded the men who had displayed conspicuous courage in three ways: with an extra share of the booty, with promotion, and with a military award or *dona militaria* (Josephus *Bellum Iudaicum* 7.14–16).

It is significant that several of the *dona militaria*, whose symbolic value was intended to replace the actual value of booty, did in fact consist of

Trajan's Column (scene XLIV): the emperor distributes rewards to auxiliary soldiers for acts of individual bravery, while their comrades praise them. Those worthy of recognition could be given an extra share of the booty and promotion. (Reproduced from Lepper-Frere XXXIV)

items that could be taken in battle. These items included torques, the symbol of the Gauls, as well as *armillae* (armbands) and *phalerae* (small discs worn on a leather chest harness). *Dona militaria* were most frequently awarded to those below the rank of *decurio*, and they were worn on parades attached to a sort of leather harness commonly depicted on funerary sculpture.

Diet

The axiom commonly attributed to Napoleon, 'an army marches on its stomach', applies to all armies of all periods, and the Roman army was certainly no exception. Certainly the best tribute to the army of the early Principate, on campaign or in peacetime or even during the rare mutinies, is that there is no recorded complaint about the Roman military diet.

Feeding the man

In peacetime the Roman soldier had a rich and a varied diet, the staple item being wheat in the form of bread, porridge and pasta. Analysis of the sewage at Bearsden, Antonine Wall, demonstrated that this diet was mainly vegetarian. Fruit included apples, pears, plums, cherries, peaches, grapes, elderberries, damsons, apricots, blackberries, bilberries, strawberries, raspberries, olives, figs and pomegranates. In addition there were nuts, such as sweet chestnuts, hazelnuts, walnuts and beechnuts. The wide range of vegetables included cabbage, garden peas, broad beans, horse beans, carrots and garlic, not to mention pulses such as lentils and chickpeas.

Even so, both literary sources and archaeology confirm that meat was also consumed. An excellent picture of the meat soldiers ate can be seen from the study of the bones that have been excavated at Roman forts in Britain and Germany. Cattle, sheep and pig were most popular, in that order, but goat, red and roe deer, wild boar, hare, fowl, fish and shellfish were also eaten. Of these supplementary commodities, seafood was very popular. A private letter to a *decurio* stationed at Chesterholm–*Vindolanda* states that the sender had received 50 oysters from a friend (*Tab. Vindol.* II 299). Cheese and eggs should not be forgotten, nor *salaria* (salt) and vinegar.

In addition *vinum* (wine) or *acetum* (sour-wine), which could be mixed with water to make the time-honoured tipple of the poor, *posca* (Plautus *Miles Gloriosus* 837, *Truculentus* 610, Suetonius *Vitellius* 12.1), and *cervesa* (Celtic beer) are all mentioned on several ink writing-tablets from Chesterholm–*Vindolanda*. One tablet, a communiqué to the garrison commander Flavius Cerialis from one of his *decuriones*, ends with the postscript: 'My fellow-soldiers have no beer. Please order some to be sent. To Flavius Cerialis, *praefectus*, from Masclus, *decurio*' (*Tab. Vindol.* III 628). That brewing itself might well have been done at or near the fort is certainly suggested by references to *cervesarii* (brewers), one named Atrectus, and to a *braciarius* (maltster) named Optatus (*Tab. Vindol.* II 182.14, III 581.4, 17, 646.2).

To sweeten their food soldiers used honey, and like many Romans they were fond of highly salted fish sauces, especially *garum*, to put on their food; *garum*, however, was very expensive, and the soldiers used a cheaper but inferior variety called *muria*.

The bathhouse at Chesters–*Cilurnum* cavalry fort. This is the changing-room (*apodyterium*); the niches in the west wall were 'lockers'. In this heated room off-duty troopers could relax with mugs of Celtic beer and platters of shellfish, and play dice or board games. (Author's collection)

Even on the fringes of the empire a number of imported foods were available to the troops. The sewage at Bearsden also contained fragments of opium poppy, dill, coriander and celery. Like olives, figs and pomegranates, these foodstuffs were most likely shipped in from the Mediterranean. The sewage also tells us that the soldiers suffered from whipworm and roundworm, and some of their grain appears to have been contaminated with weevils.

Normally two square meals were eaten each day, *ientaculum*, what we would call breakfast, and *cena* (supper). Sixth-century papyri from Egypt record a daily ration of 1.4kg (3lb) of bread, 0.45kg (1lb) of meat, 1 litre (2 pints) of sour-wine and 5cl of oil per soldier (*P. Oxy.* 1920, 2046, cf. 2013, 2014, Polybios 6.39.3). In theory, at least, each soldier was provided with a daily ration of food, which he cooked himself. The Carvoran–*Magnis* dry measure from Hadrian's Wall, however, holds the equivalent of seven daily rations (*c.*10 litres or 21 pints) and suggests that the grain was disbursed weekly. Moreover, as each trooper slept three to a barrack room or tent, it seems logical that they pooled their food, with one man taking on the cooking for the group.

Feeding the horse

Xenophon emphasizes the importance of sufficient fodder for horses so that they would be able to perform as well as required, 'since horses unfit for their work can neither overtake nor escape' (*Hipparchikos* 1.3). A horse in its natural habitat, living on grass, would eat most of the time. As a grazing animal, horses require food in small amounts frequently,

31

Barrack-block at Chesters–
Cilurnum cavalry fort, which
provided accommodation for
a *turma*. This building was
divided into ten two-roomed
accommodation units (*contubernia*),
with the inner-rooms (*papiliones*)
serving as sleeping quarters for
the troopers, and the outer-rooms
providing the stabling for their
horses. (Author's collection)

thus it is better to feed a stabled horse about three or four times a day
rather than only once or twice. Grass alone, even when supplemented by
hay in the winter months, is not sufficient for working horses since it will
not keep them in hard condition. To achieve this, extra food, usually
hard fodder in the form of cereals, must be given.

The quantity of fodder necessary to sustain each horse depends
upon its size and the amount of work it has to perform. The ratio of
cereals to hay can be varied, provided the horse always receives adequate
food-value to sustain the amount of work it is doing. Modern horses are
generally fed more hay and less cereal when they are not working. When
in work, on the other hand, horses require less roughage, so the
quantities of hay can be reduced, but require more protein so the cereal
ration is accordingly increased (Ewer 1982: 118). Oats, barley and maize
are the most commonly used modern cereals, but barley is fattening,
and slightly less barley or maize is usually given compared to oats.
Modern barley has approximately 11 per cent protein, as do oats and
maize, but varieties grown today differ very much from ancient ones
and, in the main, have far less nutritional content than ancient strains
(Hyland 1990: 40).

As ancient grains would have provided much better nutrition than
modern feeds, a smaller quantity could be fed and still achieve good

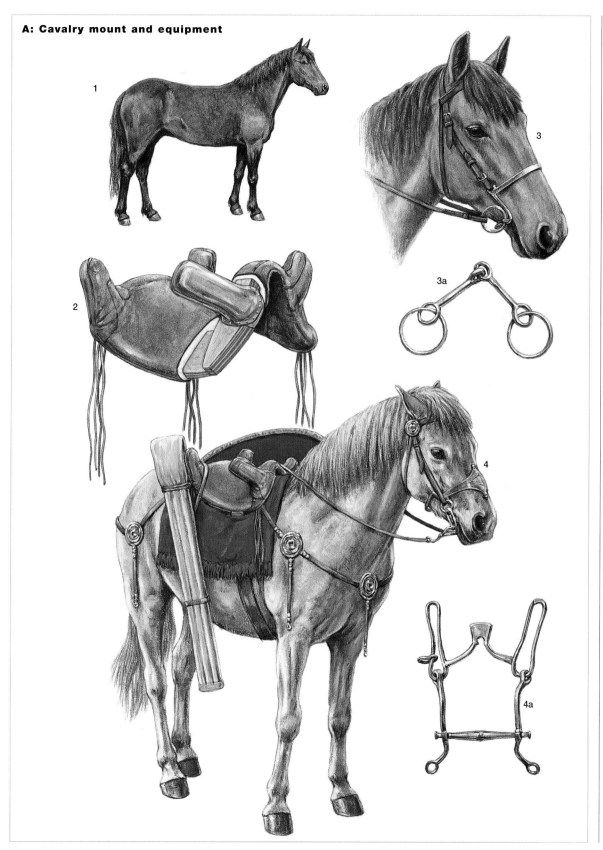

A: Cavalry mount and equipment

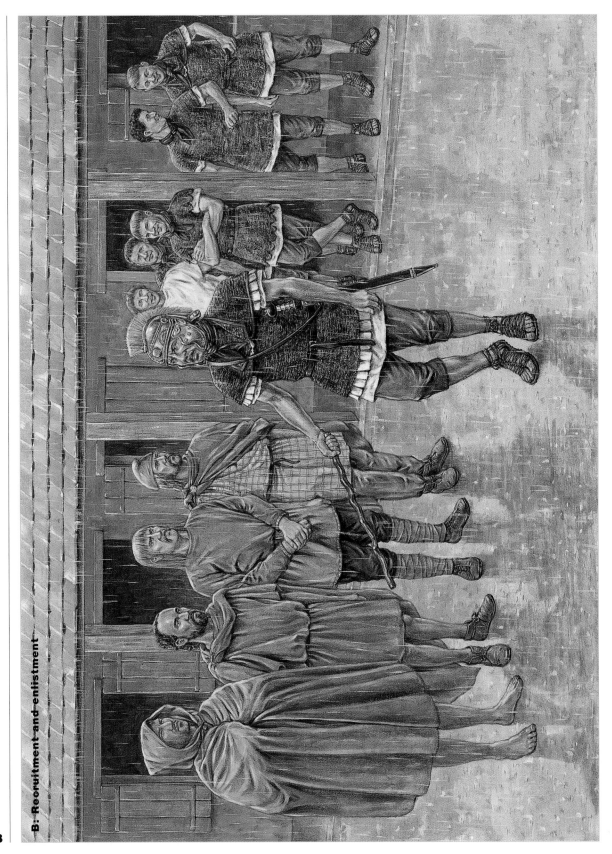

B

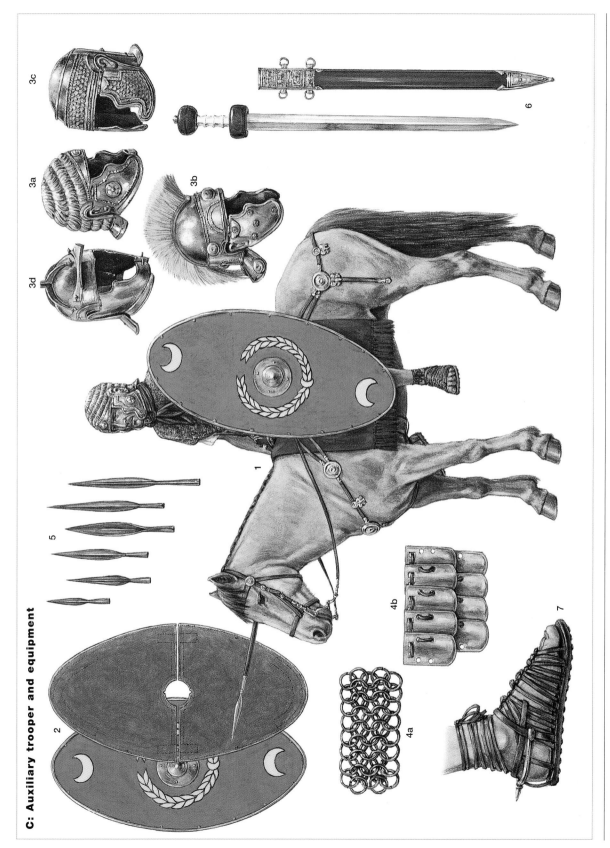

C: Auxiliary trooper and equipment

D

E

E: *Hippika gymnasia*

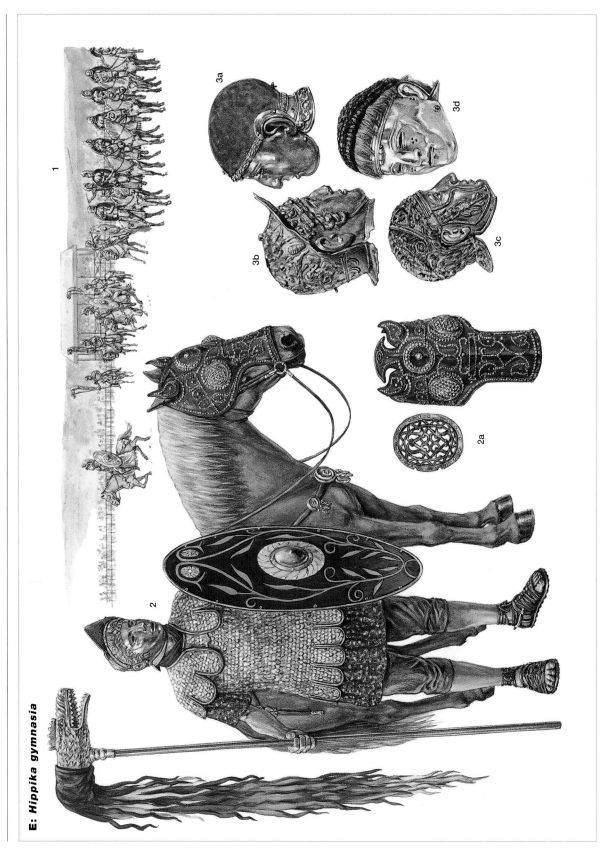

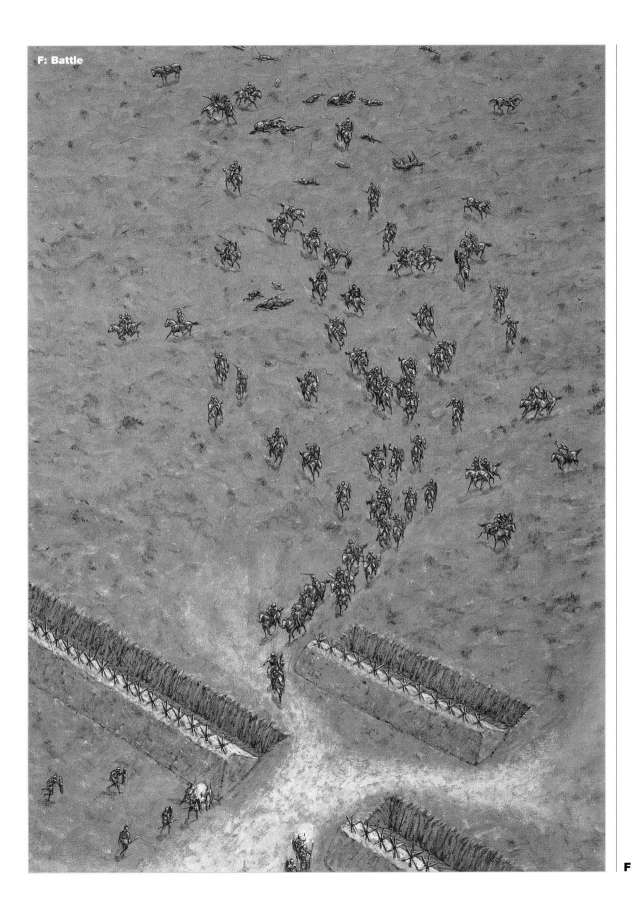

F: Battle

F

results. At the turn of the 20th century, British army cavalry horses were given a daily forage ration of 5.4kg (12lb) of hay, 4.5kg (10lb) of oats and 3.6kg (8lb) of straw, divided into three or four feeds. In addition, chaff was mixed with feeds, and bran mash was given once a week, sometimes with linseed cake (Dixon–Southern 1992: 209). A late 1st-century document from Carlisle–*Luguvalium* lists the allocation of *frumentum* (wheat) and *hordeum* (barley) to the 16 *turmae* of an *ala*. Wheat was intended for the troopers and barley for their mounts, though the latter could be used as punishment rations for the men (Suetonius *Divus Augustus* 24.2, Frontinus *Strategmata* 4.1.37, Plutarch *Antony* 39.7, Vegetius 1.13). In AD 187 a *duplicarius* of *ala Heracliana* at Coptos, Egypt, received 20,000 *artabai* of barley as the year's supply for the horses of his unit (*P. Amh.* 107, cf. *P. Oxy.* 2046). Using this evidence Davies (1989: 187) estimates that the 560 horses of a single *ala quingenaria* (including the *decurio* and *duplicarius* remounts) would eat their way through 625 tons of barley in a year.

Varro (*De re rustica* 1.31.4–5), Columella (*De re rustica* 2.10.31) and Pliny the Elder (*Naturalis historia* 18.142) all mention a mixed crop of barley, vetch and legumes, called *farrago*, Varro adding that it is good for purging horses at the beginning of spring, which is also the beginning of the campaigning season for the military. However, the evidence for cereal rations issued to the cavalry is not abundant. Polybios (6.39.13), albeit describing the military procedures of the middle Republic, confirms that men were issued with wheat and the horses were fed on a ration that was about 1.5kg (3⅓lb) dry weight of barley a day (Hyland 1990: 90, cf. Roth 1999: 64). Papyri from Dura-Europos confirm that barley formed the basis of the cereal ration for the cavalry horses of the Principate (Fink 1, 2), while papyri from Egypt show them receiving regular supplies of hay (Fink 76, 80). In truth barley is not very suitable for horses as it is apt to induce short-windedness and sweating until digestive tolerance is achieved, but it is universal in recorded antiquity until the adoption of the northern fodder-grain oats in early medieval Europe.

The hay and green fodder mentioned most often and favourably in Roman agricultural literature is what we know as lucerne or alfalfa. The Romans called it *medica* as it originated from the lush Median plain where the famed Nisaean horses were raised. Renowned for its large size, the Nisaean horse was paramount of all the breeds in the east and served as the mount of the formidable Parthian *cataphractarii* (Strabo 11.13.7). Good grass hays have a protein content ranging from 7 to 10 per cent, whereas lucerne cut at the optimum time has almost double that (Hyland 1990: 41). Columella (*De re rustica* 2.10.25) enumerates all its splendid qualities ending with the statement that the yield from 1 *iugerum* (0.25 ha) of it provides enough to feed three horses for a year. There are inscriptions referring to meadowland (*prata*) specifically set aside for the military, usually outside forts, for the grazing of cavalry mounts (*ILS* 2454, 2455, 5968, 5969, *RIB* 1049, cf. Tacitus *Annales* 13.54).

MILITARY LIFE

Foremost among the army's duties was the maintenance of law and order in the provinces. Since there was not a regular police force, much responsibility lay with the governing elite of the local cities who had only limited resources and who might in turn require the support of Roman troops not only against brigands, but against internal dissension. In many respects the Roman army was like an army of occupation. Government operations like the grain supply, tax collecting, or the maintenance of routes of communication and trade, could require a more or less permanent military presence. From this kind of activity the army's role could be extended to more routine police duties in the community.

Peacetime duties

The employment of cavalrymen can be best illustrated by examples from the military papyri. A duty roster of *cohors I Hispanorum veterana quingenaria equitata*, dating to AD 105, shows the *equites* had been despatched on various duties (Fink 63). Outside Moesia Inferior, where the unit was stationed, one trooper was in a party collecting cavalry remounts, while two others were in a garrison. A large party of 23 troopers was on a trans-Danubian expedition. Other cavalrymen had crossed the same river on an *exploratum* (reconnaissance mission) under a *centurio*. Inside the province, a *decurio* was among the *equites singulares* (bodyguards) of the governor, while another *decurio* was among a party of men watching over grain ships at a naval depot. Ironically, bandits had killed one trooper, while another had died by drowning.

Two duty rosters of *cohors XX Palmyrenorum milliaria equitata*, dating to AD 219 and AD 222 respectively, provide further information for the

Reconstructed cavalry barrack-room at Wallsend–*Segedunum*, Hadrian's Wall. This inner-room (*papilio*) would have accommodated three troopers, with their equipment, their mounts being stabled in the outer-room of the accommodation unit (*contubernium*). Note the four-horned saddle sitting on the left-hand bed. (Author's collection)

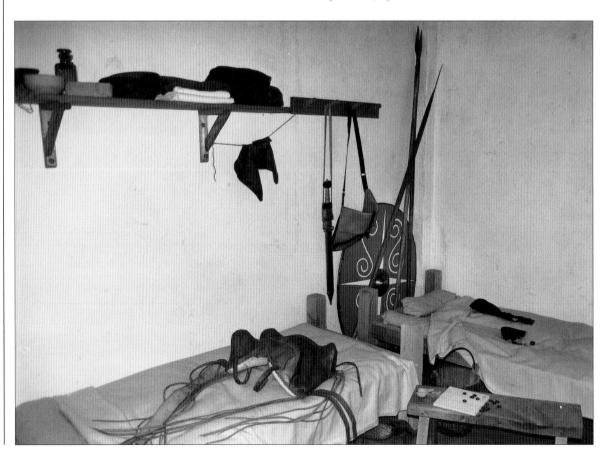

duties undertaken by cavalrymen (Fink 1, 2). Yet again, their tasks include garrison duty, *exploratores* (scouting patrols), relaying messages and despatches between bases in Syria Coele, *prosecutio* (escort duty) and serving as guards to the provincial governor, while one man is detailed to inspect horses.

Military cults

Soldiers expected special protection from a whole pantheon of powers called the *dii militares* (military gods) who aided them in their daily routine, in particular on the *campus* (parade ground), and even more so in battle. The deities worshipped by Roman soldiers may be divided for convenience into two main groups. The first group comprises the gods of the established state religions whose worship was regulated by the official calendars such as the *Feriale Duranum*. These obviously included the Capitoline triad of Iuppiter Optimus Maximus (*IOM*), Iuno Regina and Minerva, as well as the war god Mars, Victoria, the personification of victory, and the personifications of martial virtues, Disciplina and Virtus. The second group included mainly non-Roman cults that were adopted and encouraged by military units, but which were not included in the official calendars. One of the most bizarre of these cults must have been the ritual of headhunting, as practised by Gallic troopers of the Roman cavalry (Fields 2005B: 55–66). Yet Rome was tolerant and flexible with regard to deities who were not part of the established classical pantheon, and in a cosmopolitan army these were readily adopted and worshipped.

Barrack-block at Chesters–*Cilurnum* cavalry fort, with the spacious accommodation for a *decurio* that formed the base of this L-shaped building. The officer's quarters were well appointed, being equipped with hearths, washing facilities and a latrine. It also served as his office. (Photograph Esther Carré)

Dismounted Gallic troopers on Trajan's Column (scene LXXII) present the emperor with the trophies of their prowess, the severed heads of Dacian warriors. Although Rome had apparently suppressed headhunting within Gaul, it still continued to flourish on the battlefield. (Reproduced from Lepper-Frere LI)

RIGHT The Celtic horse-goddess Epona, literally 'the divine mare', on a Roman relief found in Kastel, Germany. In iconography she generally appears side-saddle on a mare and, as a patroness of horses, many of her dedicants were cavalrymen. (Author's collection)

Cult of the standards

The early Christian writer Tertullian (*fl.*AD 200) stated that the cultic system of the Roman army 'is entirely devoted to the worship of the military standards' (*Apologeticus* 16.8). Although he was exaggerating, Tertullian was not completely wrong. The cultivation of *esprit de corps* is a necessity for any military unit, and for this purpose the cult of the standards was ideal. In a very real sense, the standards formed the very identity of the unit to which they belonged and thus were revered as sacred objects. The early 3rd-century *Feriale Duranum* from Dura-Europos records the festivals celebrated in one year by *cohors XX Palmyrenorum milliaria equitata* (Fink 117). Although most of these festivals were associated with the leading deities and members of the imperial family (*dies imperii*), two days in *Maius* (May) were given over to 'the Rose Festival of the standards' (*Rosaliae signorum*) when the standards were paraded, decorated with wreaths of roses.

RIGHT The rear range in the *principia* at Chesters–*Cilurnum* cavalry fort, Hadrian's Wall. The vaulted strong room sits below the *sacellum*, the shrine in which the unit standards, statues of the emperor and the altars to *IOM* and *Disciplina* were kept. (Author's collection)

Matres campestres

A number of altars dedicated to the *matres campestres* ('mothers of the parade ground') have been found in the vicinity of forts, and are believed to indicate the site of a shrine on the *campus*. These deities are of Gallic origin, and they appear to have been worshipped exclusively by horsemen. Such altars have been found in Britain, including one from Benwell–*Condercum* on Hadrian's Wall, dedicated by Terentius Agrippa, the *praefectus* of *ala I Praetoria Hispanorum Asturum Gordiana* (*RIB* 1334). Another example is that from Newstead–*Trimontium* (*RIB* 2121) dedicated by Aelius Marcus, *decurio* of *ala Augusta Vocontiorum cR*.

Hercules Magusanus

The epithet 'Magusanus' applied to Hercules on the altar set up by Valerius Nigrinus, *duplicarius* of *ala I Tungrorum*, suggests that the Tungrian troopers stationed at Mumrills on the Antonine Wall still worshipped the classical hero in the form known to their forefathers in the lower Rhine (*RIB* 2140). His popularity with the frontier garrisons of Britannia and the

ABOVE LEFT **Altar (*RIB* 2121)
to the *matres campestres* set up
by Aelius Marcus, *decurio* of *ala
Augusta Vocontiorum cR* stationed
at Newstead–*Trimontium* during
the Antonine period. This unit had
originally been raised from the
Vocontii of Gallia Narbonensis.
(Museum of Scotland, Edinburgh;
photograph Esther Carré)**

ABOVE RIGHT **Altar (*RIB* 2140)
to Hercules Magusanus set up by
Valerius Nigrinus, *duplicarius* of *ala
I Tungrorum* stationed at Mumrills,
Antonine Wall. This cult had been
brought to the northern frontier by
troops originating from the lower
Rhineland. (Museum of Scotland,
Edinburgh; photograph Esther
Carré)**

Rhine was doubtless due to his identification with a Germanic deity,
probably Donar. Tacitus says that the Germans 'tell that Hercules, too,
once visited their country, and he is first amongst the heroes whose praises
they chant when they are about to go into battle' (*Germania* 3.1).

Hunting

Xenophon advocates hunting as an excellent form of training 'since it is
necessary that the rider should have a firm seat when riding at top speed
over all sorts of terrain, and should be able to use his weapons properly
on horseback' (*Peri Hippikis* 8.10). Since this form of exercise also
provided meat supplements to the military diet, it may have been one of
the more popular forms of equestrian practice, as is demonstrated by an
inscription that reads: 'To unconquerable Silvanus Caius Tetius Veturius
Micianus, *praefectus* of *ala Sebosiana*, on fulfilment of his vow willingly set
this up for taking a wild boar of remarkable fineness, which many of his
predecessors had been unable to bag' (*RIB* 1041). Extensively
worshipped by soldiers on the northern frontier, Silvanus was the Celtic
god of hunting and forests. The language of the *praefectus* effortlessly
reflects the spirit of the aristocratic colonial in a frontier land.

The Chesterholm–*Vindolanda* letters include references to hunting
as a leisure pursuit amongst the Roman officers commanding auxiliary

units (*Tab. Vindol.* II 233, III 593, 594, 615), and a study of the animal bones found at the fort itself indicates a far greater proportion of deer than at other Roman sites. An account (*Tab. Vindol.* II 191) of foodstuffs consumed by the household of Flavius Cerialis, the *praefectus* of *cohors VIIII Batavorum equitata* and garrison commander, includes roe deer (*capream*) and venison (*cervinam*), while a crudely cut relief (*CSIR* 389) found at nearby Housesteads–*Vercovicium* vividly illustrates a stag confronted by a hunter's net.

ON CAMPAIGN

The cavalry undertook all those roles that required mobility and speed. In most situations they provided the only available means by which actions could be carried out quickly, and, on land, the fastest and most efficient way of gaining vital information concerning enemy movements.

Rations

In peacetime, as we have seen, considerable effort was needed to provide for the army in its garrisons. During a campaign, however, the need to keep an army adequately supplied with *annona militaris* (rations) was one of the greatest concerns for a Roman commander. Vegetius

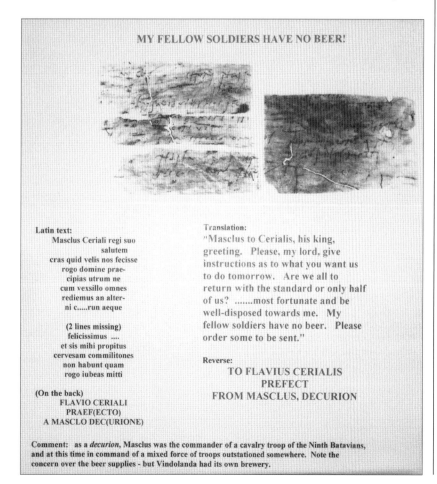

MY FELLOW SOLDIERS HAVE NO BEER!

Latin text:
Masclus Ceriali regi suo
salutem
cras quid velis nos fecisse
rogo domine prae-
cipias utrum ne
cum vexsillo omnes
rediemus an alter-
ni c.....run aeque

(2 lines missing)
felicissimus ....
et sis mihi propitus
cervesam commilitones
non habunt quam
rogo iubeas mitti

(On the back)
FLAVIO CERIALI
PRAEF(ECTO)
A MASCLO DEC(URIONE)

Translation:
"Masclus to Cerialis, his king, greeting. Please, my lord, give instructions as to what you want us to do tomorrow. Are we all to return with the standard or only half of us? ....most fortunate and be well-disposed towards me. My fellow soldiers have no beer. Please order some to be sent."

Reverse:
TO FLAVIUS CERIALIS
PREFECT
FROM MASCLUS, DECURION

Comment: as a *decurion*, Masclus was the commander of a cavalry troop of the Ninth Batavians, and at this time in command of a mixed force of troops outstationed somewhere. Note the concern over the beer supplies - but Vindolanda had its own brewery.

Facsimile of *Tabulae Vindolandenses* III 628, the ink writing-tablet written by Masclus, *decurio of cohors VIIII Batavorum equitata*, to his *praefectus* at Chesterholm-*Vindolanda*. Note the contents of the postscript, which was probably his real reason for writing to Flavius Cerialis. (Author's collection)

discusses at length the utmost importance of ensuring adequate supplies for troops campaigning in hostile territory as 'famine makes greater havoc in an army than the enemy, and is more terrible than the sword' (3.3). Hence the army placed great reliance on the pack mule, moving as fast as a man and carrying as much as a horse but eating less, whilst draught oxen were frequently employed to pull wheeled transport. The ability of oxen to remain healthy on a diet of good grass was a bonus, which compensated for their low speed.

On campaign the diet of the army was obviously less varied. Several sources speak of the iron rations a soldier carried when on campaign; these, of course, form the basic part of his diet in peacetime. This is best illustrated by Hadrian, whose policy of keeping the troops fully trained but engaged on no actual warfare is well known: 'Hadrian himself used to live a soldier's life among the other ranks and, following the example of Scipio Aemilianus, Metellus, and Trajan, cheerfully ate in the open such camp food as bacon, cheese, and sour-wine' (*SHA* Hadrian 10.2, cf. Severus Alexander 51.5, 61.2). Iron rations on active service are mentioned in connection with 2nd-century generals who are considered authoritarian, for instance Avidius Cassius, who 'forbade the soldiers when on campaign to carry anything except bacon, hardtack, and sour-wine' (*SHA* Avidius Cassius 5.3), or C. Pescennius Niger, who 'gave orders that no one was to drink [vintage] wine on campaign, but that they should be content with sour-wine' (*SHA* Pescennius Niger 10.3).

The grain ration was usually issued on campaign in the form of *bucellatum*, or hardtack (*SHA* Avidius Cassius 5.2, Pescennius Niger 10.4, Ammianus 17.8.2), what Pliny the Elder called 'old or ship's bread' (*Naturalis historia* 22.68), and Josephus (*Bellum Iudaicum* 3.95) implied was to last for three days before being ground into flour by the soldiers. This was done with a hand mill, and once turned into flour the ration was frequently baked into *panis militaris*, a type of black bread (Pliny, *Naturalis historia* 18.67). This is what the renowned orator Cicero knew as 'ration bread' (*cibarius panis, Tusculanae Disputationes* 5.97) during his soldiering days, and, according to the writer Herodian, Caracalla (r.AD 211–217) led the life of an ordinary soldier, which included baking his own bread: 'He used to eat whatever bread was available locally. With his own hand he would grind his personal ration of grain, make it into a barley-cake (*māza*), bake it in the ashes and eat it' (4.7.5). Alternatively, the ground meal could be boiled with water to make porridge or soup, the latter in combination with meat and vegetables, or turned into pasta.

Fodder

On campaign the conditions for cavalry mounts would change considerably. The animals would have to live off the land and rely on frequent foraging expeditions to provide their *capitum*. There would have been periods of plenty and, more frequently, periods of scarcity for cavalry mounts, when troopers would have become anxious over their own horse's welfare. The baggage train would only have been able to provide at best a minimal amount of cereal. The Roman cavalry horse had to be adaptable, not a fussy feeder, and its digestion able to cope with a constantly changing level of nutrition.

Before battle

While the army was marching through enemy territory it was essential for the cavalry to scout the way ahead, and to act as guards behind and on both flanks. The cavalry were the eyes and ears of the army, and as Vegetius rightly says, 'an army is exposed to more danger on marches than in battle' (3.6). Scouting horsemen could also be employed to survey the area through which the army was to march to locate the safest and easiest route to take. As Tacitus (*Historiae* 3.52.1–2) records, Antonius Primus and the other Flavian commanders despatched their cavalry on ahead to reconnoitre throughout Umbria so as to find the safest route to approach the Apennines. They could also locate potential camp sites and sources of food and water. Obviously great care was taken to gather as much information about the enemy location, strength and intentions as possible. Roman generals often went out in person to reconnoitre, as did Titus, who, according to Josephus (*Bellum Iudaicum* 5.52, 258), took picked cavalrymen. This suggests that troopers were specifically chosen for the task, presumably because of their experience and reliability.

Once the army had set up its marching camp, outposts had to be thrown forward so that any movements the enemy made could be quickly detected. The nature of the terrain dictated the type of troops selected for the duty, although in virtually all cases they would be lightly armed. In open country cavalry would be employed, whilst broken ground would require the use of auxiliary infantry. Obviously if the terrain was a combination of the two, then mounted troops would patrol the front and the flanks, so that in the event of approaching danger they could gallop back to the infantry outposts, giving them time to head back to the security of the camp. Outpost duty was clearly open to risks. However, as Xenophon instructs his reader, outposts could be used as 'snares to trap the enemy … if you conceal your outposts, you will have the chance of luring the enemy into an ambush by placing a few guards in the open to screen the hidden men' (*Hipparchikos* 4.10–12).

During battle

We do not have a manual describing the drills and tactics of the Roman army in detail, although Arrian's *Tactica* covers many aspects of cavalry tactics. The sources, however, occasionally provide some details and it appears that the Romans had an organized but uncomplicated approach to tactics. As cavalry was unsuitable to holding ground because of its tendency to advance and retreat rapidly, the tactical principles were: the use of cavalry for flank attacks and encirclement; the placing of a force in reserve; the deployment of a combat line that could maintain contact; readiness to counter-attack; flexibility in the face of unexpected enemy manoeuvres. As Napoleon succinctly put it, 'charges of cavalry are equally useful at the beginning, the middle, and the end of a battle' (*Military Maxims* 50).

An army's battle formation depended on its composition and the local terrain. For large-scale actions a favourite formation was the *triplex acies* (three lines), with auxiliary *cohortes* stationed on either side of a centre formed by the legions, and *alae* deployed on the wings with an additional force kept in reserve. This was the formation, albeit without the luxury of reserve *alae*, adopted by C. Suetonius Paulinus against

Boudicca (Tacitus *Annales* 14.37). Alternatively, the auxiliary infantry could form the first line and be supported by the citizen soldiers, as demonstrated by Cn. Iulius Agricola at Mons Graupius. Again, cavalry formed the wings, but here they were supported by more *alae* behind the main line (Tacitus *Agricola* 35.2, 37.2). However, if the enemy was overwhelmingly superior in horsemen then the Roman cavalry was either closely supported by strong detachments of auxiliary infantry or placed behind a dense infantry line. Arrian (*Ektaxis* 12–22), or Xenophon as he chose to call himself, adopted the latter battle order against the Alans, a steppe people related to the Sarmatians, whose sole tactic consisted of a headlong charge by a mass of *cataphractarii*.

Cavalry formations

Cavalry formations are somewhat obscure in our sources. The Byzantine author of the *Strategikon* (2.1), who codified the military reforms enacted by the soldier-emperor Maurice (r.586–602), recommends that cavalry, regardless of their numbers, should always be deployed in at least two lines, so that there is a reserve. He also claims that 'the Ancients' (i.e. the Romans) formed their cavalry line four deep. Josephus (*Bellum Iudaicum* 5.131) records a line of horsemen, three ranks deep, deployed behind an infantry formation. In *Tactica* (18.2) Arrian deals largely with the tactics and formation used by a double-*turma* (Greek *eile*) of 64 troopers. On

Metope I from the *Tropaeum Traiani*, depicting a cavalryman charging into battle, his *lancea* held horizontally in a relaxed position. The trooper wears a short-sleeved mail shirt and carries a hexagonal shield but, curiously, is bareheaded. (Muzeul de Archeologie, Adamklissi; Author's collection)

cavalry formations for larger units he recommends, without going into too much detail, that these should be considerably wider than they were deep (*Tactica* 16–17). Even so, a very deep formation might be employed to break through an enemy line (*Tactica* 17.3).

Horse versus horse

When the army deployed for battle it was the infantry who were expected to form up in the centre to fight the main action and deliver the crushing blow. However, the success of the cavalry in protecting the flanks and defeating the enemy cavalry could decide the outcome. The cavalry of the Principate employed a mix of skirmish and shock tactics and was effectively trained and equipped for both. Arrian, in his description of the *hippika gymnasia*, devotes four chapters in the *Tactica* (36–39) to the use of the javelin: 'throwing their javelins in as heavy and continuous a rate of fire as possible' (36.3), 'they must carry as many javelins as they can throw … provides nothing more than a continuous rate of fire and incessant din' (37.1). Of course, the short-shafted lightweight javelin used here would only be accurate over short distances; the heavier *lancea* would have been more accurate, albeit with a shorter range.

As horses refuse to collide into an oncoming line of horsemen, encounters between opposing cavalry units would have been very fluid, fast-moving affairs. When combats occurred, it was either because the two lines had opened their files, allowing them to gallop through each other's formation, or they had halted just before contact, at which point individuals would walk their mounts forward to get within weapon's reach of the enemy.

The cavalry of the Principate was highly confident, and, because it was well trained and led, was able to rally more easily after a pursuit or flight and keep its formation. The author of the *Strategikon* (3.11) points out that it is not dishonourable for cavalry to take flight, provided that they return to the combat. Cavalry combats could sway to and fro as each side beat the enemy, pursued them, and were in turn beaten and pursued by fresh enemy troops. Normally the victor was the side that kept a formed, fresh reserve the longest.

Horse versus foot

Cavalry were not normally expected to charge well-ordered infantry, as the results would have been mutually catastrophic to the opposing front ranks. Besides, a horse, especially one being ridden, will not in normal circumstances collide with a solid object if it can stop or go around it. Tacitus (*Historiae* 4.33) describes loyal Roman cavalry refusing to charge home on a solid line formed by the rebel Batavian cohorts.

Cavalry, therefore, would employ typical skirmishing tactics, that is, riding up, shooting, wheeling away, and then rallying ready to try again. Arrian describes these tactics against a simulated infantry target in the *hippika gymnasia*:

> Charging straight on, they veer to the flanks, as if turning in a circle. Their veering is to the right, that is, to the spear. Thus nothing stands in the way of the javelin throwing and, in the charge, shields have been set over those throwing. (*Tactica* 36.5)

Such practice was important, for it is difficult to hit a stationary target, let alone a moving one, when the firer is shooting from a moving horse. Thus, whilst the speed of his mount made a firing horseman a difficult target to hit, the horse's irregular motion made his own aim uncertain.

The object of shooting at an enemy infantry unit was to weaken it, so that it would be unable to withstand a mounted charge. Many *alae* under the Principate carried *lancae*, but were still armoured and equipped for close combat. Outside Ascalon the poorly armoured Jewish rebels were quickly reduced by the *lancae* of the Roman cavalrymen to a state in which they could not stand up to a charge (Josephus *Bellum Iudaicum* 3.13–21).

Pursuit

As Napoleon said, 'it is the business of the cavalry to follow up the victory, and to prevent the enemy from rallying' (*Military Maxims* 51). Hence when the battle had been won, the cavalry naturally came to the fore, pursuing and harrying the broken foe. Again Arrian describes these tactics in another exercise of the *hippika gymnasia*: 'Next they draw their *spathae* and to the best of their ability make one stroke after another, to come up in pursuit of a fleeing enemy, to cut down a fallen one, to perform any stroke on the flank while riding alongside him' (*Tactica* 43.3, cf. Josephus *Bellum Iudaicum* 5.61–62). This is where the horns of the military saddle would have made the use of the *spatha* very much more effective. The trooper could ride hard, secure in his saddle as his horse twisted and turned underneath him. Such security enabled him to put all his energies into his sword strokes, lean further out of his saddle to cut at the fleeing foe directly in front of him, or, by hooking his opposite thigh under the front horn, lean out at an angle to either side in a downward thrust at a fallen one. However, during a pursuit horses became blown and vulnerable to fresh enemy reserves. The Romans, therefore, were careful to leave a part of their available cavalry in reserve.

Metope VII from the *Tropaeum Traiani* shows a trooper holding the freshly decapitated head of a Dacian warrior. It appears that Gallic members of the Roman army were still practising the Iron Age warrior tradition of headhunting. (Muzeul de Archeologie, Adamklissi; Author's collection)

AFTER SERVICE

All veterans could look forward to a relatively privileged status in comparison with the rest of the lower orders of Roman society, since they were exempt from certain taxes and personal services, and immune from some punishments, such as being condemned to the mines or to the arena. Furthermore, there were benefits that came with long and satisfactory service and eventually with *honesta missio* (honourable discharge) itself. Auxiliaries received citizenship for themselves and their existing children, and their *conubium* with one woman was recognized even if she was non-Roman; although it did not make the wife a citizen, it meant that future children would be citizens.

Discharge and retirement

Roman citizenship appears to have been awarded before the time of Tiberius, although under this emperor it may have begun to be given after a fixed term of 25 years' service. The system became fully developed under Claudius when the right of *conubium* was given in conjunction with the granting of citizenship. The regularization of this grant resulted in the issuing of *diplomata* (a modern term), which consisted of a pair of bronze tablets, tied together with wire.

Diplomata were distributed directly by the emperor and were inscribed on the front with a list of units stationed in the same province who also had men in their ranks who had served for 25 years, the recipient's name and that of his commanding officer, together with a date. A list of witnesses was engraved on the back. To prevent forgery, the text was duplicated on the insides of the plates, before being tied and sealed, so that if there was any doubt of its authenticity, an official could check to see if the seal had been broken, and then inspect the details inscribed within.

These *diplomata* were not certificates of honourable discharge as they were issued to auxiliary soldiers simply as verification of having served 25 years. Additional certificates specifically recording discharge are known, and one wooden example from Fayum, Egypt, belonging to a cavalryman, reads as follows:

In the consulship of Manius Acilius Aviola and Pansa [AD 122], on the day before the nones of *Ianuarius* [4 January], Titus Haterius Nepos, the Prefect of Egypt, gave a honourable

Dismounted Gallic troopers on the Column of Marcus Aurelius (scene LXVI) present severed heads to an otherwise disinterested emperor. From the style of their dress it appears these are members of the emperor's mounted bodyguard, the *equites singulares Augusti*. (Author's collection)

discharge (*honesta missio*) to Lucius Valerius Noster, time-expired *eques* of *ala Vocontiorum*, from the *turma* formerly commanded by Cavius. [Signature of prefect] I read that which is written above and gave a honourable discharge on the day before the nones of *Ianuarius*. (*ILS* 9060 = Campbell 321)

Such documents were not standard issue to soldiers and would be acquired by men who needed proof of their status so that they could claim the privileges awarded to veterans. It is known, for example, that in Egypt an examination called the *epicrisis*, which was conducted by officials selected by the prefect, had to be endured by a veteran if he wished to settle here. Since soldiers often married local women this acted as an incentive to remain in the province where they had served. No similar examination, however, is known outside Egypt, which, after all, was an exceptional province controlled personally by the emperor, not through a senatorial legate, but through an equestrian prefect. Egypt was of considerable strategic and economic importance, and senators were not even allowed to visit the province without the emperor's permission (Tacitus *Historiae* 1.11).

Honourable discharge could be granted to a soldier, but only after a thorough medical examination, before he had completed his 25 years if he had been seriously wounded, or was considered too weak or ill to complete his term of service. This type of discharge (*causaria missio*) still allowed a man to gain rewards he would have received had he completed his 25 years. The privileges available on honourable discharge to an auxiliary did not include a grant of land in a military colony or money, as it did for a legionary. He did, however, gain immunity from taxation and the opportunity to hold municipal office and, of course, Roman citizenship.

Dishonourable discharge (*missio ignominiosa*) was the penalty for soldiers committing a serious crime. Such men were barred by law from living in Rome itself, or from entering imperial service in any form (*Digesta* 49.16.13.3), and may have been branded or tattooed with a symbol of ignominy (*Codex Iustinianus* 12.35.3). In addition they enjoyed none of the rights and privileges granted to soldiers honourably discharged at the end of their service.

Death and burial

Death in service from combat, disease or natural causes was an inescapable possibility. The army, therefore, guaranteed every soldier, regardless of rank, a decent burial. Burial clubs are attested for the legions at least, and Vegetius (2.20) states that a compulsory deduction was made from a soldier's pay. Documentary evidence for burial clubs comes from pay-roll accounts, such as that of Proculus serving in Damascus (Fink 68), who made an annual contribution of 4 *drachmae* (equivalent to 4 *denarii*) to the fund (*ad signa*).

Soldiers killed in battle were normally collectively cremated or buried under mounds near the scene of conflict. If a soldier died whilst in garrison, however, he would most likely be buried outside the post in which he was stationed. After death it was customary for the body to be washed, anointed and finally dressed ready for a period of lying in state. The funeral that followed began with a procession in which the deceased, lying on a funerary couch, was carried on a bier to the place of burial. In civilian life the bearers were male relatives or friends. In the army, however, fellow soldiers would have performed this duty. When the funeral procession arrived at the place of interment the burial rites were performed. The corpse and the couch were lifted on to a pyre and the body burnt. After the cremation the ashes and burnt bones of the body were collected together and poured into a receptacle for burial. These containers could be of stone or marble, silver or bronze, but more common were glass vessels and ceramic jars. If the body was to be inhumed, on the other hand, it was placed in the ground protected either by a coffin of stone, wood or lead, or a simple cover of terracotta tiles; sometimes it had no protection beyond the customary linen shroud.

After the funeral a banquet took place at the grave. This *silicernium* (feast), in honour of the dead, was followed by another, the *cena novendialis*, eaten on the ninth day after the funeral. At these ritual meals it was considered that the *di manes* (spirits of the dead) were somehow able to join their living relatives to enjoy the food and drink provided.

Cavalry tombstones

While the literary sources provide a framework for the history of the Roman army, inscriptions in general furnish additional information. Moreover, inscriptions also have an advantage over the literary sources in that they generally mean what they say. The text is usually quite short: the name of the deceased and his military unit, perhaps the number of years served and the age at death. Sometimes the inscription may be accompanied by a full-length sculptured representation of the deceased in uniform, seen as he wished to be remembered by his comrades and future generations. Such depictions, which were fashionable in the 1st century, are important to our understanding of the development of equipment and weaponry.

The tombstones, erected along the roads leading away from fortresses or forts, marked the last resting-place of the body – or more usually the ashes – of the deceased. Naturally tombstones cost money, and not everyone could afford them: rank and wealth, therefore, are to a great extent reflected in funerary expenditure. It is doubtful that the burial club paid for more than the most rudimentary of markers for the grave, and it is noteworthy that over 50 per cent of the figured military tombstones of the 1st century from Britain and Germany show mounted troops of some sort (Bishop 1988: 114). A simple memorial meant that the ashes might simply be placed in a glass jar or an earthenware pot, with a wooden marker, or none at all, at ground level. A soldier who had conscientiously saved money during his service years independently of the unit burial club, would have ensured proper commemoration if the need arose. Many tombstones state that a man's heirs, in accordance with his will, erected them.

On military tombstones the soldier's name is usually followed by his rank, for example *miles* (soldier), *veteranus* (veteran), *centurio* (centurion), *decurio* (decurion), *eques* (trooper), or *duplicarius* (*turma* second-in-command). The use of the sign '7' for the word 'centurion' or 'century' is frequently employed. Next appears the name of his unit, such as *legio II Augusta* or *ala I Thracum*, followed by his age at death, as in *annorum XXV* (aged 25), and his length of service expressed in the number of annual remunerations received as, for example, *stipendiorum XXII* (of 22 years' service). Some things are rarely mentioned on a soldier's tombstone, such as the cause of death.

Most cavalry tombstones show a named trooper at his military best and kitted out with regulation cavalry equipment of helmet, body armour, shield, one or two spears and a sword. His horse has a four-horned saddle with a short, fringed, utilitarian saddlecloth, the bridle is sometimes plain, but more often has *phalerae*, as does the harness. The horse's mane frequently has the forelock braided or tied in a poll-knot, whilst the tail can be bound. A common type (*Reiter*) of funerary sculpture depicts the deceased cavalryman riding a rearing horse and brandishing his weapons as one or more semi-naked 'barbarians' cower beneath its prancing hoofs. The other common type (*Totenmahl*) depicts the dead man enjoying a funerary banquet in the afterlife in the upper scene, whilst his horse is paraded in all its equipment in the lower. Usually the horse is being controlled from behind by means of long reins, whilst the *calo* (horseman's groom) carries spare *lancae*.

RIGHT **Tombstone of Longinus, who is depicted wearing *lorica squamata* and carrying an oval *clipeus*. His *spatha* is not visible, presumed to be on the left hip. The decorated horse harness is conspicuous, likewise the fringed saddlecloth. (Colchester and Essex Museum; Author's collection)**

Tombstone of Titus Flavius Bassus, who died aged 41 after 26 years' service as a trooper in *ala Noricorum*. He is depicted in the classic posture of the victorious cavalryman, galloping his horse over a vanquished 'barbarian'. (Römisch-Germanisches Museum, Cologne; Author's collection)

The tombstone of Longius at Colchester–*Camulodunum* (*RIB* 201 = Campbell 45) is in the form of a *Reiter* relief bearing a mounted cavalryman in action, a type of stele common to auxiliary troopers serving in the provinces of Germania and Britannia. This example is the earliest surviving cavalry tombstone from the new province of Britannia, all of which belong to the 1st century, and probably dates to the Claudian period. Colchester–*Camulodunum* was a legionary fortress from the conquest in AD 43 until AD 49, when its garrison, *legio XX Valeria*, was transferred to a new base at Gloucester–*Glevum* to campaign against the Silures. Longinus was a Thracian from Sardica (Sofia, Bulgaria). As he was a non-citizen (Longinus would have gained this on his discharge, had he survived 25 years' service in the *auxilia*) he lacks the three-part name, or *tria nomina* (*praenomen* – *gentile nomen* – *cognomen*) common to Roman citizens. Furthermore Longinus is not described as a *veteranus* and, therefore, must have been a serving soldier when he died. The inscription on his tombstone reads as follows:

LONGINVS SDAPEZE / MATYGI F(ILIVS) DVPLICARIVS / ALA PRIMA THRACVM PAGO / SARDI(CA) ANNO(RVM) XL AEROR(VM) XV / HEREDES EXS TESTAM(ENTO) [F(ACIENDVM)] C(VRAVERVNT) / H(IC) S(ITVS) E(ST)

'Longinus, son of Sdapezematygus, *duplicarius* from the First *ala* of Thracians, from the district of Sardica, 40 years old, of 15 years' service. His heirs had this set up in accordance with his will. He lies here.'

GLOSSARY

The following provides much of the terminology, both military and equine, associated with the Roman cavalry of the Principate. In most cases both singular and plural forms are given.

acetum	sour-wine
ad signa	compulsory deduction from pay to burial club
adlocutio	speech to troops
ala/alae	cavalry 'wing'
annona militaris	rations
armilla/armillae	armband – military decoration
artaba/artabai	Egyptian grain measure (= 18 litres)
bars	gums between horse's molars and incisors
barding	horse armour
breeching	leather harness-strap around horse's rump for saddle
bucellatum/bucellata	'hardtack'
calo/calones	groom
campus/campi	parade ground
cantle	rear of saddle
capitum	fodder
capsa/capsae	field-dressing box
capsarius/capsarii	'paramedic'
cataphractarius/ cataphractarii	heavily armoured cavalry
cena	evening meal
cervesa	Celtic beer
chamfron	head armour for horse
cohors equitata/ cohortes equitatae	mixed auxiliary cohort of foot and horse

57

contus	heavy spear held two-handed
decurio/decuriones	*turma* commander
denarius/denarii	silver coin (= 4 *sestertii*)
diploma/diplomata	certificate issued to auxiliary on discharge
dona militaria	military awards
duplicarius/duplicarii	**1.** double-pay **2.** *turma* second-in-command
epistrophai	wheeling 90 degrees
eques/equites	trooper
exercitator/exercitatores	riding instructor
explorator/exploratores	mounted scout
focale/focalis	woollen scarf
frumentum	**1.** grain **2.** wheat
garum	quality fish sauce
gyrus	training-ring
hackamore	metal horse 'muzzle' (Arabic *hakamāh*)
hand	unit (= 4 inches) for measuring horse's height
hippika gymnasia	cavalry sport
honesta missio	honourable discharge
hordeum	barley
imaginifer	bearer of *imago*
imago/imagines	standard bearing image of the emperor
ientaculum	breakfast
lancea/lancae	light-spear
long-reins	means of driving horse from behind
lorica hamata	mail armour
lorica squamata	scale armour
magister campi	equestrian drill instructor
milliaria/milliariae	'one-thousand strong'
missio causaria	medical discharge
missio ignominiosa	dishonourable discharge
modius/modii	Roman grain measure (= 9.1 litres)
muria	inferior fish sauce
panis militaris	military bread
pereginus/peregrini	non-roman citizen

petrinos	equestrian manoeuvre adopted from Celts
peytral	horse's breast band
phalera/phalerae	**1.** military award **2.** disc-junction
praefectus	*ala* commander
pratum/prata	military meadowland
principales	subordinate officers of *turma*
probatio	examination for new recruits and remounts
prosecutio	escort duty
pteruges	leather fringing on armour
quingenaria/quingenariae	'five-hundred strong'
sacramentum	oath of loyalty
sagittarius/sagittarii	archer
sesquiplicarius/sesquiplicarii	**1.** pay-and-a-half **2.** *turma* third-in-command
sestertius/sestertii	brass coin (= $^1/_4$ *denarius*)
signaculum/signacula	identity disc
singulares	bodyguards
spatha/spathae	cavalry sword
stipendium/stipendia	**1.** pay **2.** period of service
strator/stratores	inspector of remounts
tiro/tironis	recruit
torque/torques	neckband – military decoration
toloutegon	equestrian manoeuvre adopted from Celts
turma/turmae	sub-unit of an *ala*
umbo/umbones	shield boss
undones	woollen socks
vexillarius/vexillarii	bearer of *vexillum*
vexillum/vexilla	cavalry standard
vitis	vine-rod
xynema	equestrian manoeuvre adopted from Celts

Inscription (*RIB* 1463) from Chesters–*Cilurnum* cavalry fort recording the bringing of water (*aqua adducta*). This was put up by *ala II Asturum* during the governorship of Ulpius Marcellus (*c.*AD 177–184), and probably relates to a new water supply for the bathhouse. (Author's collection)

DEDICATION SLAB RECORDING THE SUPPLY OF WATER TO THE SECOND ALA OF ASTURIANS, WHEN ULPIUS MARCELLUS WAS GOVERNOR

CHESTERS 1897

Abbreviations

AE	*L'Année Epigraphique*, Paris (1888–)
BAR	*British Archaeological Reports*, Oxford
Campbell	B. Campbell, *The Roman Army, 31 BC – AD 337: a Sourcebook*, London, (1994)
CIL	T. Mommsen *et al.*, *Corpus Inscriptionum Latinarum*, Berlin (1862–)
Fink	R.O. Fink, *Roman Military Records on Papyrus*, New Haven (1971)
ILS	H. Dessau, *Inscriptiones Latinae Selectae*, Berlin, (1892–1916)
Lepper-Frere	F. Lepper and S.S. Frere, *Trajan's Column: a New Edition of the Cichorius Plates*, Stroud, (1988)
P. Amh.	B.P. Grenfell and A.S. Hunt, *The Amhurst Papyri*, London (1900–1901)
P. Oxy.	B.P. Grenfell, A.S. Hunt and H.I. Bell *et al.*, *The Oxyrhynchus Papyri*, London, (1898–)
Tab. Vindol. II	A.K. Bowman and J.D. Thomas, *The Vindolanda Writing-Tablets* II, London (1994)
Tab. Vindol. III	A.K. Bowman and J.D. Thomas, *The Vindolanda Writing-Tablets* III, London (2003)
RIB	R.S.O. Tomlin, *Roman Inscriptions of Britain²* (Stroud, 1995)
SHA	*Scriptores Historiae Augustae*

BIBLIOGRAPHY

Anderson, A., *Roman Military Tombstones*, Shire, (1984)

Bishop, M.C., 'Cavalry equipment of the Roman army in the 1st century AD', in J.C. Coulston (ed.), *Military Equipment and the Identity of Roman Soldiers*, BAR International Series 394, 67–195, Oxford (1988)

Le Bohec, Y., (trans. R. Bate), *The Imperial Roman Army*, Routledge, London (1994, 2000)

Bowman, A.K., *Life and Letters on the Roman Frontier: Vindolanda and its People*, British Museum Press, London (1994, 2003)

Connolly, P., 'The Roman saddle', in M. Dawson (ed.), *Roman Military Equipment: the Accoutrements of War*, BAR International Series 336, 7–28, Oxford (1987)

Cichorius, C., (revised by J.E.H. Spaul), *Ala²: the Auxiliary Cavalry Units of the pre-Diocletianic Imperial Roman Army*, Nectoreca Press, Andover, (1994)

Feugère, M., (trans. D.G. Smith), *Weapons of the Romans*, Tempus, Stroud (2002)

Fields, N., 'Dexileos of Thorikos: a brief life', *Ancient History Bulletin* 17, 108–126 (2003A)

Fields, N., *Hadrian's Wall, AD 122–410*, Osprey (Fortress 2), Oxford (2003B)

Fields, N., *Rome's Northern Frontier, AD 70–235*, Osprey (Fortress 31), Oxford (2005A)

Fields, N., 'Headhunters of the Roman Army', in M. Wyke and A. Hopkins (eds.), *Roman Bodies: Antiquity to the 18th Century*, Papers of the British School at Rome, London 55–66 (2005B)

Davies, R.W., *Service in the Roman Army*, Edinburgh University Press (1989)

Dixon, K.R. and Southern, P., *The Roman Cavalry, from the First to the Third Century AD*, Batsford, London (1992)

Ewer, T.K., *Practical Animal Husbandry*, John Wright & Sons, Bristol (1982)

Goldsworthy, A.K., *The Roman Army at War, 100 BC – AD 200*, Clarendon Press, Oxford (1996, 1998)

Goldsworthy, A.K., *The Complete Roman Army*, Thames & Hudson, London (2003)

Hyland, A., *Equus: the Horse in the Roman World*, Batsford, London (1990)

Hyland, A., *Training the Roman Cavalry: from Arrian's* Ars Tactica, Sutton Publishing, Stroud, (1993)

Hyland, A., *The Horse in the Ancient World*, Sutton Publishing, Stroud (2003)

James, S., *Excavations at Dura-Europos 1928–1937, Final Report VI: the Arms and Armour and other Military Equipment*, British Museum Press, London (2004)

Keppie, L.J.F., *The Making of the Roman Army, from Republic to Empire*, Routledge, London (1984, 1998)

Nobis, N., 'Zur Frage römerzeitlicher Hauspferde in Zentraleuropa', *Zeitschrift für Säugertierkunde* 38, 224–252 (1973)

Roth, J.P., *The Logistics of the Roman Army at War (264 BC – AD 235)*, Brill, Leiden (1999)

Summer, G., *Roman Military Clothing (1), 100 BC–AD 200*, Osprey (Men-at-Arms 374), Oxford (2002)

Watson, G.R., *The Roman Soldier*, Thames & Hudson, London (1969, 1985)

COLOUR PLATE COMMENTARY

A: CAVALRY MOUNT AND EQUIPMENT

(1) Horses of 14 to 15 hands would have been quite adequate for military purposes. The lack of stirrups tended to limit the desirable size of mounts, even if larger animals were available; riders had to vault into the saddle from the ground, clearing the tall saddle-horns. This is quite feasible, even in armour, with moderate-sized horses, as reconstructions have shown.

(2) It has long been known that Roman saddles had four tall horns and Peter Connolly's reconstruction, duplicating in all details the archaeological and iconographic evidence, demonstrates the arrangement of these. The rear pair stands vertical, and secures the rider's rump, while the front pair angle outwards, effectively hooking over the rider's thighs and holding him firmly in place.

(3) The strength and speed of horses need to be controlled; the bridle and bit play a vital part in exercising that control. The horse's sensitive mouth means that it responds to very slight pressure from the bit.

(3a) The iron snaffle bit consists of a jointed bar with a ring on either end. The bar is placed in the horse's mouth and the reins are attached to the rings. Celtic in origin, this type of bit is less harsh on the horse's mouth than the Roman curb bit.

(4) Romans preferred robust, rounded horses, unsurprising considering the loads these animals had to carry. Here a cavalry mount is fully equipped with bridle, harness, saddle, saddlecloth, trooper's shield and javelin quiver. Hyland estimates the total load of the Roman cavalry horse as 38.5 kg exclusive of the rider (1990: 154). Note a hackamore is fitted over the horse's muzzle to prevent it opening its mouth and resisting the curb bit.

(4a) The Roman curb bit from Newstead–*Trimontium* is very severe, and was clearly designed to give the rider full control with one hand. The tongued bar is placed in the horse's mouth, while the open bar is positioned under the horse's chin, enabling the rider to pull the animal's head sharply upwards, thus giving him greater control. The ring (two originally) is for the attachment of the bridle straps, and the eyes for the reins.

B: RECRUITMENT AND ENLISTMENT

A *decurio* inspects newly arrived recruits while a group of off-duty troopers look on. He carries the vine-rod (*vitis*), which serves as the mark of his rank and as a means of inflicting punishment. 'So let the adolescent who is to be selected for martial activity', says Vegetius, 'have alert eyes, straight neck, broad chest, muscular shoulders, strong arms, long fingers, let him be small in stomach, slender in buttocks, and have calves and feet not swollen by surplus fat but firm with hard muscle' (1.6). The physical characteristics of these ethnically diverse recruits certainly do not match Vegetius' ideal type.

The basic article of clothing for both military and civilian use was the tunic, usually white or off-white. This was a sleeveless woollen garment made of two rectangular pieces of cloth sewn together and closed with seams under the arms and down the sides. The seams were left un-sewn either side of the neck and held together by a bronze pin. Unbelted, the tunic would reach to mid-calf, but it was usual to blouse it out over a belt worn at the waist. Civilians would thus adjust their garment to below the knee, but it was a mark of a soldier to wear it much higher, at mid-thigh level. Soldiers would also have been recognizable by their hobnailed boots (*caligae*) and suede breeches (*bracae*) worn to mid-calf. Juvenal (*Satura* 3.248, 16.24–25) warns civilians about encountering a soldier with his *caligae*, and advises against provoking them as they might kick their shins in retaliation. Note three of the recruits wear leather slipper-like boots, while one is bare-foot.

The bare-foot recruit wears a form of coarse woollen hooded cloak (*paenula*), commonly worn by everyone, soldiers and civilians, in inclement weather. Invariably of a yellow-brown hue, the body was cut from a single piece of cloth, to hang with a straight lower edge. It was fastened down the front, to mid-chest level, with two button-and-loop fastenings and two bone or wooden toggles. A pointed hood was sewn on separately. Two others wear heavy woollen cloaks fastened at the right shoulder by means of a bronze brooch. This is the *sagum*. Of Celtic origin, this garment was especially popular with the military and was worn by all ranks from the emperor down.

Two of the four copper-alloy plates for reinforcing the horns of a Roman saddle, from Newstead–*Trimontium*. These are front plates, and are inscribed with the name of the owner, 'SIINIICIO', 'Senecio', which suggests saddles were tailor-made. (Museum of Scotland, Edinburgh; photograph Esther Carré)

LEFT **Trajan's Column (scene CXLII) shows auxiliary troopers wearing military cloaks (*saga militaria*) fastened at the right shoulder. Apart from the obvious use of keeping the wearer warm, the heavy woollen *sagum* was doubtless used on campaign as a groundsheet or blanket. (Reproduced from Lepper-Frere CIV)**

BELOW **Auxiliary troopers crossing a river on Trajan's Column (scene XXI). A short-sleeved mail shirt, with scalloped edges, is clearly seen on the cavalryman negotiating the pontoon bridge, likewise the knotted scarf (*focale*) around his neck to prevent chafing. (Reproduced from Lepper-Frere XVI)**

C: AUXILIARY TROOPER AND EQUIPMENT

(1) This mounted trooper, fully armed and equipped for battle, represents a cavalryman from the time of Trajan's Dacian wars. Though manufactured in the early part of the 1st century, his helmet is of auxiliary cavalry type 'A', while his short-sleeved mail shirt is based on those worn by troopers on Trajan's Column. In addition he has a woollen scarf (*focale*) tied around his neck to prevent chafing from the mail shirt.

(2) The plywood shield is a *clipeus*, the flat, oval type common to cavalrymen. The shield-board is covered in rawhide and edged in bronze. Attached to it by

four rivets is a hemispherical copper-alloy boss. The shield is provided with a soft leather cover, probably of goat hide, to prevent it from becoming waterlogged and warped. It is based on the well-preserved oval shield covers from Valkenburg, Netherlands, while the painted shield design is taken from Trajan's Column.

(3a) This iron plate helmet is of auxiliary cavalry type 'A', represented by an almost complete example from Weiler near Arlon, Belgium. Dating to the first quarter of the 1st century, this helmet is probably the earliest true Roman cavalry combat headpiece and has a 3mm-thick skull piece with a thin bronze sheet, embossed with stylized human hair, applied over it. The brow edge is fitted with a finely decorated applied bronze strip, and the cheek-pieces are finished with a thin bronze skinning.

(3b) This iron plate helmet, with applied bronze skinning, is of auxiliary cavalry type 'B', represented by a specimen found at Witcham Gravel, England. Dating to the second quarter of the 1st century, this type has a slightly larger nape-guard than its predecessor, and is ornamented with six large bronze bosses and five small bosses per cheek-guard. Crests were almost certainly not worn in battle, except possibly by *decuriones*.

(3c) This bronze-skinned iron helmet is based on that found at Butzbach, Germany. The feather pattern is of Thracian origin, and the piece was probably manufactured during the third quarter of the 1st century.

(3d) The formidable iron plate helmet is of auxiliary cavalry type 'E', introduced at the turn of the 2nd century. The skull piece has crossed reinforces of bronze secured with conical rivets, while the deeper nape-guard affords far more protection to the trooper's neck against a back-hand sword cut; the flanged cheek-guards, which hook together at the chin, give better defence to the throat than earlier patterns. This headpiece could bear a horsetail crest.

(4a) Roman mail seems to be of a standard construction in which each ring passes through four others, two in the row above and two in that below, but it was very laborious to make. The problem was partly overcome by the introduction of alternate rows of punched rings, which did not need to be joined; hence a riveted ring was interlinked with four punched rings. The 'rivet' to secure the flattened ends of riveted rings was a small triangular chip of metal, closed with a pair of tongs with recessed jaws.

(4b) The scales, which appear always to have been of a single metal and usually of a single size on a given garment,

Iron spearhead from Newstead–*Trimontium* bearing the inscription 'T TVN T BA': '*turma* of Tun … *turma* of Ba …' Troopers 'labelled' their equipment with the name of their *decurio*; in this instance the *turma* appears to have changed commanders. (Museum of Scotland, Edinburgh; photograph Esther Carré)

were attached to each other in rows by copper-alloy wire that passed through a vertical pair of holes in each lateral edge. The ends of the wire were bent or hammered over at the back. The completed rows were then attached to the fabric backing, usually by heavy thread. This thread was sewn through a vertical pair of holes in the centre of the top of the scale.

(5) *Lancae* commonly had what are today loosely termed 'leaf-shaped' spearheads. These were most likely manufactured in generalized sizes and shapes, there being no standard typology of spearheads in the Roman army. The various types of spearhead were all made from iron that was left untempered, which not only reduced production time, but also allowed for on-the-spot field repairs to be carried out by the soldier.

(6) The hilt of the *spatha* comprised three separate components: grip, guard and pommel. Grips, made of bone, ivory or wood, were deeply grooved to fit the four fingers of the hand. Pommels tended to be elliptical in shape, and were made from wood, ivory or bone. Guards were semi-oval and rectangular, and made from iron, copper alloy, wood or bone. Surviving scabbards are either plain wood or wood covered in leather. Made from bone, ivory, copper alloy or iron, the locket (top) and the chape (bottom) were designed to provide decorative protective ends to the scabbard. Decoration could take the form of engraving or inlaying.

(7) The standard form of military footwear for all troop types, *caligae* consisted of a fretwork upper, an insole and a sole. The sole was made up of several layers of leather glued together and studded with iron hobnails. The one-piece upper was laced up the foot and ankle with a leather thong, the open fretwork providing excellent ventilation that would reduce the possibility of blisters. This *caliga* is equipped with a prick-spur secured by straps.

D: TRAINING

The basic aim of training is the creation of that ephemeral quality, *esprit de corps* – a soldier's confidence and pride in himself and his unit. Personal bravery of a single individual does not decide the issue on the actual day of the battle, but the bravery of the unit as a whole rests on the good opinion and the confidence that each individual places in the unit of which he is a member. Vegetius says (1.27) that Roman cavalry trained, fully armed and divided into their *turmae*, on 20-mile (32km) marches three times a month. Under the watchful eyes of the *decuriones*, they practised equestrian evolutions, pursuit, retreat, counter-charging, all conducted on varied terrain so horses and men could work in both flat and rough country.

Set at the time of Agricola's campaigns in Caledonia, this reconstruction shows a *decurio* putting his *turma* through its

paces. His dress and equipment were mostly the same as those of troopers, though of better quality cloth and more ornately decorated; as a mark of his rank he wears his *spatha* on the left side and carries a vine-rod (*vitus*). Equally, his helmet has a fore-and-aft crest, and his horse has a woollen neck strap and fringed peytral of soft leather.

The four-horned saddle and harness can be seen here. As the rider sat down, his weight caused the horns to close around and grip his thighs, so allowing him to lean either side without losing his seat. It is secured with a breast strap, haunch straps and breeching, and a girth that passed through a woollen saddlecloth. These leather straps are linked by niello-inlaid bronze, tinned-bronze or silver disc-junctions (*phalerae*), and decorated with non-functional brass pendants.

E: HIPPIKA GYMNASIA

(1) Set at the end of Hadrian's reign when Arrian wrote his *Tactica* (AD 136), this scene shows the *hippika gymnasia*, an elaborate ritual where Roman cavalry practised manoeuvring and missile handling. These displays took place on the garrison's extramural parade ground with the participants and their mounts wearing highly decorative 'sports' equipment. Such spectacles not only impressed visiting dignitaries, but also encouraged the cavalrymen to maintain their equestrian skills and built morale.

(2) This cavalryman is a *draconarius*, named after his *draco* or dragon standard. Originally a 'barbarian' standard of Sarmatian origin, the open mouth of the hollow, bronze dragon's head allowed the wind to fill the tapering tubular tail, while giving out an audible hissing sound (Arrian *Tactica* 35.3–4). He wears the archetypal piece of sporting equipment, the 'face-helmet' with a highly decorative skull-piece and the cheek-guards replaced by a solid facemask with holes for the eyes, nose and mouth. It is possible these helmets were intended to represent the 'enemy' in the *hippika gymnasia*, but equally they could just be reflecting a style used in the workshops where they were manufactured.

(2a) This horse bears a leather-studded chamfron like that found at Newstead–*Trimontium*, which not only enhanced its appearance, but also protected the animal, as is evident from the dome-shaped bronze grilles that shield the eyes but still permit vision.

(3a) This silver-plated iron sports helmet from Emesa, Syria, represents one of the earliest examples (cavalry sports type 'A'). Running along the neckband is an exquisite scroll decoration, while the mask appears to depict the face of an oriental.

(3b) Late 1st-century bronze sports helmet found near the fort at Ribchester–*Bremetennacum*, England. The prominent peak that projects from a highly decorated skull-piece distinguishes

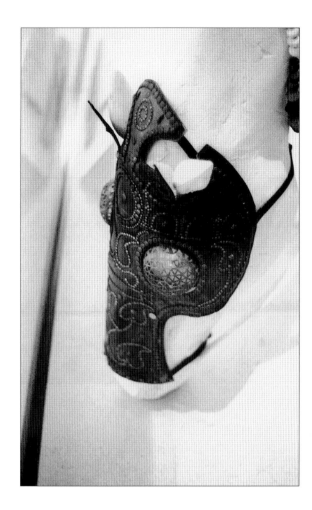

A richly decorated leather chamfron, which is a modern reconstruction of the example found at Newstead–*Trimontium*. Although direct evidence is lacking, this reconstruction has been equipped with bronze eye-guards of an openwork design. (Museum of Scotland, Edinburgh; photograph Esther Carré)

this helmet type (Cavalry Sports type 'B'). The skull piece of this example features embossed reliefs of fabulous beasts and warriors fighting.

(3c) Mid-1st-century bronze sports helmet from Vize, Bulgaria. The helmet (cavalry sports type 'D') was either completely or partially silvered.

(3d) Sports helmet from Nijmegen–*Noviomagus*, Netherlands, presenting a variation on the common style of having the skull-piece shaped to represent wavy hair. In this case, real animal hair has been fixed to the helmet instead. This type of helmet is characterized by the mask depicting a youthful face.

F: BATTLE

A conjectural reconstruction depicting the aftermath of the civil war battle of Second Cremona (24/25 October AD 69), the critical engagement that decided the outcome of the 'Year of Four Emperors'. Here the victorious Flavian cavalry is hotly pursuing the fleeing Vitellian cavalry who are attempting to reach the safety of their camp outside the town of Cremona. The camp had been built at no great distance from the walls and suburbs of Cremona on the north-east, between the converging road from Brixia and the Via Postumia, and near their junction. In their hurried pursuit the Flavians are spaced out, not laterally through the fields, but along the road.

The main battle was fought through the night, with victory going to the Flavians as dawn broke: at first light *legio III Gallica*, a crack Syrian legion, turned to salute the rising sun in their customary way and this created rumours of reinforcements, heartening the Flavians and striking dismay into the Vitellians (Tacitus *Historiae* 3.24.3–25.1). This nocturnal phase of the engagement, despite the full moon, had been a confused and bitter affair and, as Tacitus says, 'on both sides weapons and uniforms were the same, frequent challenges and replies disclosed the watchword and standards were inextricably confused as they were captured by this group or that and carried hither and thither' (*Historiae* 3.22.3). A civil war creates stronger passions and tends to produce shocking events, and the climax of Second Cremona was to be no exception. When the main (southern) gate of the camp was finally forced, the surviving Vitellians threw themselves down from the ramparts and took shelter in nearby Cremona. Despite a show of surrender, the inhabitants of this affluent town fell victim to indiscriminate rape and slaughter. A signal atrocity had occurred in this final phase – the killing of a father by his son (Tacitus *Historiae* 3.25.2) – and the sack of a Roman town by Roman troops would send a thrill of horror through the empire.

G: AFTER THE BATTLE

Medical personnel were attached to the legions and *auxilia*, and the most important of these were skilled doctors (*medici*), often of Greek origin, perhaps on a short commission and having the status and pay of an equestrian officer. Some military doctors were called *medici ordinarii*, and it is possible that they had a long-term commission with a rank and status equivalent to that of a *centurio*, though not tactical command. There were other junior medical attendants and orderlies, some of whom were also designated *immunes*, that is, 'exempt from more onerous duties' (*Digesta* 50.6.7). These men will have possessed a sound basic knowledge and skill in medical matters.

The men who provided more rudimentary treatment than the senior medical personnel were known as *capsarii*. They were so called because of the round bandage-box (*capsa*) that they carried, containing the bandages and dressings. Their primary task in the field was to patch the wounds, and get the wounded back to a medical tent as quickly as possible. That they were proficient is evident from Trajan's Column (scene CIII), which shows a legionary being helped to the field dressing-station by an orderly and a comrade, while an auxiliary trooper is having a thigh wound dressed by a *capsarius*. The latter has cut away the trooper's breeches and is swathing the limb in a bandage, holding it in his right hand and unrolling it as he works from left to right.

Here a cavalryman, wounded in a battle during one of Marcus Aurelius' Danubian campaigns, is receiving medical treatment from a *capsarius*. In the background soldiers are busy scouring the battlefield for loot. Although frowned upon by the military authorities, looting was commonplace when soldiers were expected to pay for equipment from their wages.

INDEX

Figures in **bold** refer to illustrations